UFOs

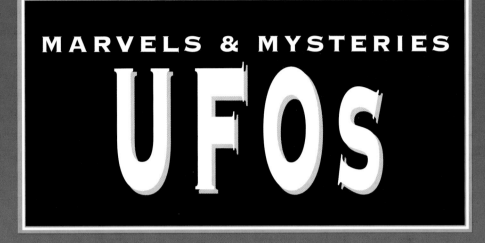

MARVELS & MYSTERIES
UFOs

PARRAGON

This material has previously appeared in
partwork form as *The Unexplained*

Published in 1997 by Parragon
Unit 13-17 Avonbridge Trading Estate,
Atlantic Road, Avonmouth, Bristol BS11 9QD

ISBN 0-7525-1227-7

Printed and bound in Italy

CONTENTS

INTRODUCTION

The first reports of flying saucers were made in the 1940s, when the term was coined. Wartime airmen claimed they were being buzzed by swift-moving, bright but apparently insubstantial craft they christened 'foo fighters'. However, these were not the first unidentified objects to appear in the skies. Two articles in this book look back to earlier this century, when there were scores of reports of unusual aeroplanes and airships. It was not until science fiction books and novels had familiarized people with the idea of interplanetary travel, and the Nazi war machine had put rockets into production, that people began to see spacecraft. The intriguing possibility arises that people 'see' what they know, rather than what is really there. Perhaps, in the days before aeroplanes or indeed hot air balloons, UFOs were identified as strange birds or supernatural beings such as angels.

The nature of UFOs – indeed their very existence – is surrounded by controversy. It is a subject which seems to attract fraudsters and the occasional crank, but the activities of such people should not blind us to the fact that a real phenomenon, whatever its nature, is being reported by many others. This book presents an objective look at the evidence – including detailed illustrated accounts of a few selected encounters and a number of spreads of challenging photographs – and at some of the theories which have been formulated to explain it, and invites you to make up your own mind, or, better still, to leave it open. It also presents you with practical advice on watching for, recording and reporting UFOs for yourself.

CLASSIC ENCOUNTER

THE OBJECT IN A FOREST CLEARING HAD THE APPEARANCE OF A CLASSIC 'FLYING SAUCER' – AND ITS EFFECTS ON THE ELDERLY FORESTER WHO CAME UPON IT WERE TERRIFYING

To be of interest to a ufologist, an object must be more than merely unidentified: it must also be of 'high strangeness', as the jargon has it. Thus, a flashing white light passing overhead may be unidentified: but if there is nothing exceptional about it, there will be no reason to suppose that it is other than a conventional aircraft. However, if it wobbles rapidly in its flight, it must be regarded as 'strange', and the UFO researcher will be intrigued. Sceptics claim that 'strange' UFO cases invariably turn out to be based on unreliable evidence, while the most reliable cases have simple, 'non-strange' explanations. But the case of the Livingston UFO encounter will confound them, for it is both 'strange' and based on reliable evidence.

The Livingston case is classed as a close encounter of the second kind – meaning that the UFO was seen at close quarters and interacted with the environment. In fact, it also left evidence of its visit and physically affected the witness. Because of the high quality of the data, the case will almost certainly become a classic.

Livingston is a new town, 13 miles (21 kilometres) west of Edinburgh in Scotland. The town is generously spread over the rolling West Lothian landscape, so there are many trees and much open space. A forest adjoins the Glasgow-Edinburgh motorway at the northern edge of the town. The scene of the extraordinary events is a small clearing in this forest, only 110 yards (100 metres) from the motorway, but not within sight of it. Access to the clearing, via back roads and forest tracks, is difficult.

PRELUDE TO THE INCREDIBLE

The only witness to the encounter was Robert Taylor, then 61 years old. At the time, he was employed as a foreman forester by Livingston Development Corporation, which managed the forests through its own Forestry Department. Taylor, a quiet and phlegmatic Scot, had spent his entire life in forestry. He had a reputation for honesty and plain dealing, and was regarded by his employers as utterly reliable. He was married, with several grown-up children. He had heard of UFOs, but took no interest in them.

For reasons that will become clear later, we must record his state of health. Like many older people, he suffered from angina and high blood pressure, possibly as a result of atherosclerosis (incipient hardening of the arteries). He had undergone two minor operations and suffered two serious diseases. In 1965, he had viral meningitis, from which he made a good recovery; and in 1977, he suffered mild hepatitis. He had no history of head injury and did not normally suffer headaches, dizziness or blackouts – although, a few months before the incident, he complained of severe headaches for which no cause could be found. His hearing was good and he needed spectacles only for reading.

The artist's impression, above, shows the weird sight that astounded forester Robert Taylor, at Livingston, Scotland, as marked on the map, below.

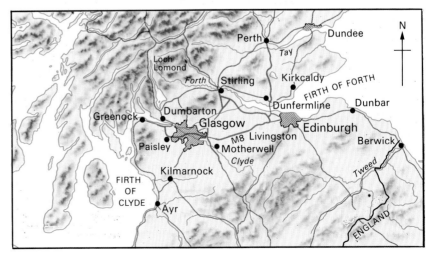

Although he drank alcohol occasionally, he did not do so during working hours.

The encounter occurred on Friday, 9 November 1979. As usual, Taylor went home for his mid-morning break at about 9.30 a.m. He was on his way back to work by about 10 a.m. He drove a Forestry Department pick-up truck and was accompanied by Lara, his Irish setter. His purpose that morning was to check that sheep had not wandered into any of the forests and that all gates were secure. He drove the truck as far as he could down a narrow track and parked it; thereafter, he had to walk. Lara was exploring among the trees and was out of sight as Taylor rounded a corner into the clearing at about 10.15 a.m. There he stopped in amazement.

Sitting on the ground, or hovering just above it, in the centre of the clearing, was a large object. It was shaped like the upper half of a sphere, with a rim or flange at the 'equator'. It was about 20 feet (6 metres) across. The lower hemisphere was not visible, or was non-existent. There was neither visible movement nor audible sound.

The object was a dark grey-buff colour, later likened by Taylor to the colour and texture of emery paper. But, periodically, different parts changed in

Robert Taylor is seen, below, standing in the clearing where he suffered his traumatic encounter with three mystery objects. His boss said of him: 'Bob Taylor is not a man to make something up. If he says he was attacked by some creatures, then there must have been something there.' But the case would probably have been quickly forgotten had inexplicable markings on the ground not been found at the site of the encounter.

appearance to become transparent or reflective. Protruding from the upper edge of the flange were several regularly spaced stems, surmounted by what looked like propellers, although they did not rotate. Just above the rim on the surface of the hemisphere was a series of circular patches that were even darker than the surrounding surface. No other features were visible. Taylor immediately concluded that the object was a spacecraft.

Almost at once, perhaps as a response to his arrival, Taylor was approached by two smaller objects that seemed to come roughly from the direction of the 'spacecraft'. Each object was a sphere, between 1½ and 3½ feet (50 centimetres – 1 metre) in diameter and was the same colour and texture as the larger object. Attached to each sphere were several protrusions or 'legs' sticking out in all directions, and it was on these that the spheres rolled rapidly towards Taylor. He noticed that, as each 'leg' touched the ground, it made a sucking or plopping noise. Taylor was overwhelmed by a pungent smell, which he likened to that of burning brake linings; it nearly choked him. The spheres stopped, one on each side of him, and each attached a 'leg' to the legs of his trousers, just below the pockets. Almost at once, he felt the

spheres pull him forwards towards the 'spacecraft', tugging him by his trousers. Struggling for breath and trying to resist the pull of the spheres, he lost consciousness and collapsed.

ALARMING SYMPTOMS
When Taylor regained consciousness, he was alone except for Lara, who was barking in concern for her master. The strange objects had all disappeared. When he tried to speak to the dog, he found that he had lost his voice. When he tried to stand, he discovered that his legs would not support him. He had a frontal headache and a strong thirst, and he felt sick. He was still aware of the foul smell as a taste in his mouth, and his chin was sore.

Taylor crawled on all fours for about 100 yards (90 metres) back along the forest track before he was able to stand up. He then continued, walking unsteadily, until he reached the truck. He realized that he ought to report the event to his office over the two-way radio, but still lacked speech. He tried to reverse the truck, but it ran off the track into soft ground and became stuck. Consequently, he had to walk home (his house was nearer than the office), a distance of just over a mile (1.8 kilometres), via a short cut through fields and woods. His voice returned while he was on the journey home. He arrived about 11.15 a.m.

When Mrs Taylor saw her husband's dirty face and clothes, and heard him mutter that he had been attacked by a 'spaceship thing', she wanted to call their doctor, but was restrained by her husband. He took a bath, but still complained of the smell, although his wife could not detect it. She telephoned Malcolm Drummond, head of the Forestry Department, who in turn notified a doctor, Gordon

Physical traces left after the UFO incident at Livingston – disturbances of the earth and grass – can be seen in the photographs above. There were a number of circular holes, above left, arranged in twin circles. Fresh soil was exposed in each of these holes. The other markings consisted of a pair of ladder-like patterns in which the 'rungs' were short, parallel indentations in the grass, above right. The ground beneath was not affected.

Adams. Drummond arrived at the house first and immediately interviewed Taylor in his bath. Taylor explained what had happened and insisted that there must still be marks on the ground where the 'machine' had 'landed'. Drummond dashed up to the woods but could find no marks.

Meanwhile, Taylor – now out of his bath – had told the doctor: 'You're not going to believe this story!' Dr Adams examined Taylor but found very little wrong with him. He did have a slight graze under his chin and another on his left thigh, but there was no sign of head injury or brain compression, although he still had a headache. His temperature, blood pressure, heart and lungs were normal. The doctor wanted a head X-ray made, as well as a psychiatric report, and he telephoned for an ambulance to take Taylor to nearby Bangour General Hospital. Meanwhile, he allowed him to accompany Drummond and other Forestry Department personnel back to the forest. When Taylor showed his colleagues where the 'spaceship' had stood, they now all saw strange marks in the grass. This area, about 25 by 20 feet (7.5 by 6 metres), was immediately fenced off and the police were informed.

Mr and Mrs Taylor went by ambulance to the hospital, but they were kept waiting for about two hours. Because they had planned to visit relatives in England over the weekend, Robert Taylor discharged himself without being examined.

Mrs Taylor had already noticed that her husband's trousers were torn, and all the clothing he had been wearing was later taken by the police for forensic examination.

So many people now knew of the incident that it was inevitable that the press would be informed, and all Britain heard of the encounter when the story was carried by the *Sunday Express* on 11 November. ('Forester "attacked by visitors from space"'). The most sensational report was that of *The Sun* on 12 November, which claimed that 'space thugs' had attacked Taylor and his dog, and that Taylor had been left cut and bleeding!

Investigations of the incident were conducted both by the Lothian and Borders police, and the British UFO Research Association. The police investigation quickly established that there was no obvious or simple explanation. The markings in the grass were not connected to any others – in fact, there were no others in the area – and there was no sign that any vehicles had recently driven through the area. One officer even conducted a fruitless search for signs of a mobile crane that might have been used to drop an object into the clearing! No helicopter activity had been reported; in any case, the marks were not those of a helicopter. The police could find no rational explanation for the marks, nor for any other aspect of Taylor's story; yet they found no reason to question his honesty.

Forensic examination of Taylor's trousers showed that the holes in them were tears – not cuts or burns – caused by some broad attachment pulling the material upwards.

There were also some anomalous small holes associated with the tears. A hole in his long johns coincided with one of the trouser tears, as did the graze on Taylor's thigh.

The ground markings at the encounter site have been sketched out in the plan, below. The circular, broken line represents the size and position of the UFO, as estimated from Robert Taylor's account. Each of the circular holes slopes into the ground. In the diagram, the rim of each hole is shown as a full circle, while the crescent-shaped shading shows the sloping side of the hole. Could a complex pattern of electrical discharges have been responsible for creating these markings?

Taylor was asked if he could have torn his clothing on the way home that day. But there was no need for him to jump fences or struggle through undergrowth on the route he took.

The markings on the ground were the next object of investigation. Even more compellingly than Robert Taylor's account and the injuries he had suffered, they testified that something extraordinary had happened in the forest clearing that day.

MYSTERIOUS TRACKS

The day after Robert Taylor had been 'attacked' by mysterious objects in that forest clearing near Livingston, Scotland, the odd ground marks described by Taylor were still visible, although they were not easy to make out among the tufts of coarse grass. They were of two types. First, there were two isolated parallel 'tracks', each about 8 feet (2.5 metres) long and the same distance apart. Each 'track' was 1 to 1½ inches (2–3 centimetres) wide and deep, and about 1 foot (30 centimetres) long. The grass between the indentations was evenly flattened.

Everyone had assumed that the 'tracks' had been made by some heavy object – for example, a caterpillar tractor (presumably endowed with the power of flight, since the 'tracks' began and ended abruptly). But they were a feature of the grass only; the ground beneath was not altered in any evident manner.

Surrounding the 'tracks' were many holes where the earth had been exposed. Each was about 4 inches (10 centimetres) across and the same in depth. They were roughly circular, and nothing about them identified them as having been made by any particular tool. Nor was the earth in the holes compressed. Each hole was angled into the ground at about 30° from the horizontal. All 40 of the holes were mapped by the police. Two distinct rings of holes were evident on their plan, and the direction at which they were angled into the ground changed gradually and consistently around each circle: if one regarded one of the rings as circulating clockwise, then the other circulated counterclockwise. The rings were adjacent between the 'tracks', so that the holes were paired.

Robert Taylor insisted that there was no machinery or equipment in the clearing during the previous month, even though new water mains were being laid only 110 yards (100 metres) away. It did not seem likely that the holes were made with a pick. Samples of soil were taken, both from one of the holes and from nearby, but no significant difference between them was found.

Accurate timing of the morning's events revealed that Taylor must have been unconscious for about 20 minutes. That is a period much greater than would be expected if he had merely fainted, so some sort of more complex cause must have been responsible. Medical experts advised the UFO investigators that only two possible mechanisms presented themselves. One is a stroke, but that ought to have left Taylor with either a one-sided weakness or neurological damage. The other possible cause is an epileptic attack. This might explain the length of unconsciousness, which would include a period of sleep after such an attack, the loss of control of the vocal cords and limbs, the

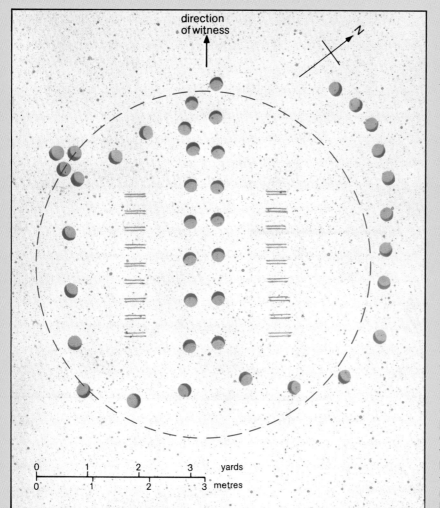

direction of witness

N

0   1   2   3   yards

0   1   2   3   metres

headache and the nausea. It would even explain the pungent smell and the very sighting of the UFO, for a characteristic of many epileptic attacks is that, during the preceding 'aura' – the strange sensations that precede unconsciousness – the victim has various hallucinatory experiences, and a strong, unpleasant smell is very common.

It should be noted that meningitis, from which Robert Taylor had suffered, damages the cerebral cortex and renders its sufferers more prone to epilepsy than would otherwise be the case. An electroencephalograph examination of Taylor showed normal brain behaviour, but that proves very little; epileptics may indeed show normal brain activity between attacks.

Some have concluded that the UFO must have been a machine of some kind and that the spheres were robots, which either accidentally or deliberately grabbed Robert's clothing. But it is extremely unlikely that it was a man-made machine: no such device is known to exist. Others, however, are certain that the UFO *was* an alien spaceship.

But there could be an alternative explanation. According to this hypothesis, the objects were a form of ball lightning. The dark colour and protrusions are unusual, but by no means unknown, in ball lightning, and thought to be caused by atoms of carbon. Protrusions that have occasionally been reported – in this case, the 'legs' – might represent the poles of an octopolar (eight-poled) magnetic field. (The more familiar magnetic field of a bar magnet has two poles.) The holes in the ground might have been caused by electrical discharges, like miniature lightning strikes. And the 'tracks' could be evidence of a very powerful magnetic field, also thought to be present when ball lightning occurs.

Indeed, Taylor may have been caught between two powerful magnetic fields. Acting together, they could have placed a strong field across his brain. Although there is no experimental work to support this idea, it seems probable that such a field could gravely disturb the normal electrical operations of the brain, especially in someone whose brain had been damaged by meningitis. Taylor, remember, experienced an extremely unpleasant smell, marking the beginning of what may well have been an epileptic fit.

According to Taylor's description, the UFO was larger than most ball lightning, but experts are not agreed on what the maximum size of ball lightning can be, although some put it at 20 to 23 feet (6 – 7 metres). The object's equatorial rim could have been a distortion caused by rotation; and the 'stems' rising from the rim may have been magnetic flux tubes connecting the ball lightning to the surrounding magnetic field of the Earth.

There was no thunderstorm in the area that day. But instances of ball lightning on thunder-free days are well documented. Ball lightning is a largely unknown phenomenon, but it may explain many UFO reports – even, perhaps, close encounters of the second and third kinds.

PERSPECTIVES

CHANGING ROUND

The object seen by Robert Taylor is reminiscent of a UFO witnessed by a certain Herr Krauss as he walked along a road in Germany. This sphere rolled along beside him for a distance of about 165 yards (150 metres). At one point, it lowered a tube with which it apparently drew up water from the roadside. As it did so, part of its central portion changed colour, taking on a milky appearance, while the outer part took on a bluish tinge 'like the ionized air to be seen around electrical generators'. Then the tube was withdrawn and the sphere rolled past Krauss into a field and vanished skyward so fast that he could not follow it with his eyes. The object's spokes, though described by the case investigator as 'probably telescopic', suggest the eight poles of a complex magnetic field, which some believe could also account for the Livingston object.

Experts are also confounded as to whether a spherical shape seen in Germany – as illustrated right – was a 'nuts and bolts' spacecraft or some form of electrical phenomenon.

axis
of
rotation

'hosepipe'

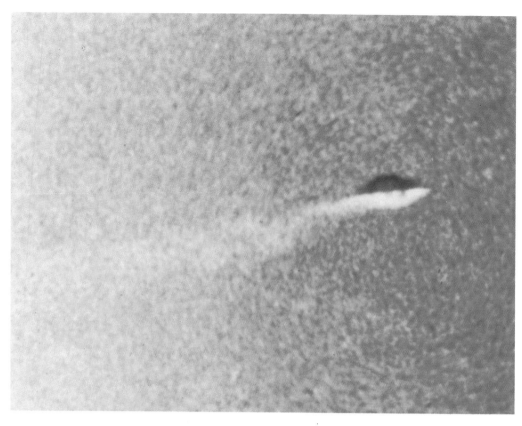

The daylight disc, left, has an unusual feature – an apparent trail of smoke streaming behind it.

The phenomenon, below, is known as an 'airglow' – luminescence of the sky at night. Odd enough to be taken for a UFO, it is actually caused by atoms in the upper atmosphere, releasing energy absorbed from solar radiation.

MAKING A UFO REPORT

IF YOU SEE AN UNIDENTIFIED FLYING OBJECT, WHAT SHOULD YOU DO, AND WHOM SHOULD YOU TELL ABOUT YOUR SIGHTING?

In July 1978 a middle-aged couple in Manchester saw a brilliant red cog-wheel float across the sky. They thought they had seen a UFO. Not knowing anything about the subject, they wrote to Patrick Moore, the astronomer, whose programmes they had watched on television. Perhaps they did not express themselves fully and Patrick Moore did not question them in depth. In any event, he advised them that what they had seen was probably a meteor, albeit a spectacular one. The couple thought no more of the matter until, six months later, they happened to watch a programme in which a well-known UFO investigator appeared.

They contacted her and related their story. Whatever it was they had seen, it was now clear that it was not a meteor. The object had been too large, and had been seen in daylight for several minutes. (Meteorites usually remain visible for only a few seconds.) What they had experienced, according to the UFO investigator, was an impressive close encounter of the first kind: and it was only by chance that their valuable eyewitness report was not lost forever.

FOBBED OFF

Two years earlier, just a few miles from this sighting, Detective Sergeant Norman Collinson of the Manchester police force was returning from duty in the early hours of the morning when he saw a strange white disc in the sky. Naturally, he reported his sighting to what he believed to be the 'proper authorities' and waited for a reply, if not an explanation. He was told by his superiors, to whom he had reported the incident, that his account would be passed on to the Ministry of Defence. But, despite

course, if you have a camera within reach, use it! It is surprising how many people who are perfectly equipped to take photographs are so overwhelmed by what they have seen that they fail to do so. If it is dark, and there is a controlled shutter speed on your camera, set it for a reasonably long exposure – probably about one second. This offers a much better chance of recording what may be a relatively dim phenomenon, even if it appears to the eye to be reasonably bright.

If you are in a car, switch on the ignition and, if you have one, the radio. There are enough stories to support the belief that some UFO phenomena can cause interference with electrical systems; and

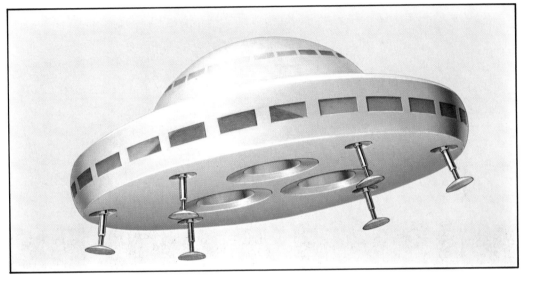

Many UFO reports describe craft that are much more complex than a simple, featureless 'flying saucer'. The drawing, right, shows a number of details that crop up in sighting after sighting – but how much detail would you remember if this UFO flashed by at high speed? Try drawing it from memory in 24 hours' time and check how much you have recalled accurately. It is a technique requiring practice.

several attempts to get an answer, Collinson heard no more. Frustrated by this, he contacted his local university, but received only non-committal replies to his questioning. When he asked for the address of the local UFO group, for example, he was told, 'Oh... you don't want to bother with them'.

But with persistence, Collinson did contact such a group. As it turned out, not only was his case a valuable addition to the evidence for the UFOs, but Collinson became a keen UFO investigator himself.

Both these cases illustrate the importance of what can happen after someone has sighted a true UFO. But, as both these cases also show, it is not always easy to find out who is the right person to contact. So if you have seen something strange in the sky, what should you do?

OTHER WITNESSES

If you believe that what you have seen might be a true UFO, first of all it is important to try to find corroborative witnesses. It is not, however, advisable to knock on people's front doors – some may not take too kindly to your intrusion. This does not mean that you should not try to call the attention of those close by. Their presence may add weight to your sighting, or they may be able to provide some other explanation of the phenomenon you have seen. It could, after all, simply be an identified flying object (or IFO).

Another important step is to make notes about the environment and the area in which the sighting is made. Factors such as the barking of dogs or the sudden silence of birds may be significant. Of

such evidence can be extremely important to your eventual report.

FLOATERS

As you watch the 'thing' in the sky, try a couple of quick experiments. Move your head from side to side and watch what happens to the UFO. This will help to eliminate one claim commonly made by disbelievers – that pieces of dead matter in the eye's optical system, known as floaters, are often taken to be UFOs. If a floater is the cause, the 'UFO' will move as your eyes move.

Secondly, try willing the UFO in a particular direction! This may sound ridiculous, but there is a

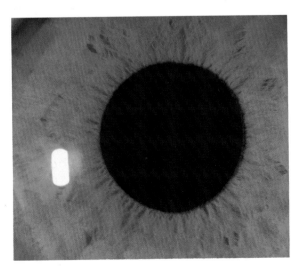

According to one theory, 'floaters' – pieces of dead matter in the eye, right – are sometimes mistaken for UFOs.

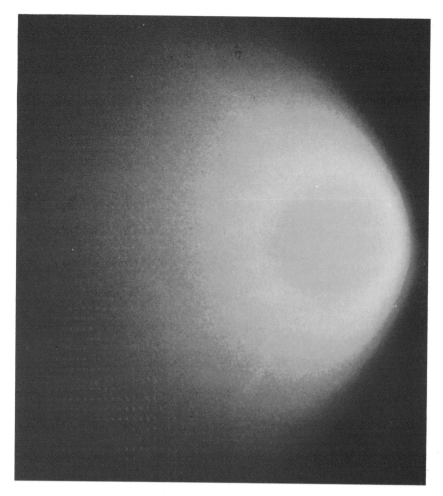

The weird light, above, is a barium cloud, launched into the upper atmosphere as part of an investigation of the Earth's electrical and magnetic fields conducted by NASA. While bodies like NASA tend to deny the existence of UFOs, they can in fact help identify unusual but explicable phenomena that appear in the skies.

school of thought that says UFOs are related to psychic phenomena. If this is so, then it should be possible for a witness to exert some degree of control over them. Interesting evidence may conceivably emerge from this exercise.

EYE FOR DETAIL

UFO encounters rarely last for long, and there is unlikely to be the opportunity to telephone anyone while the object is still in view. Time is better spent taking in as much detail as possible. This is a skill that improves with practice. Look at the picture of the 'UFO' on page 85 for about a minute. Then, tomorrow, try drawing it from memory in as much detail as possible, without cheating by looking at the original. Try the same experiment with various other UFO illustrations, varying the length of time from as little as an hour to as long as a week between examining the picture and redrawing it. The importance of being able to recall in detail what you have seen is paramount, and requires practice.

After the UFO has disappeared, do not discuss details of what you have seen with anyone else who might be around. Simply exchange telephone numbers and addresses, just as you would if you were involved in a road accident. Agree with other witnesses on who is to report the sighting and to whom. Finally, advise all the witnesses that, at the first possible opportunity, they should draw the object you have all seen, and write out a statement describing the sighting. Each witness should do this independently, and not talk about it to anyone else until they have done so. It is surprising how easy it

is to be unwittingly influenced by what others say.

To whom should you report your UFO sighting? There are several possibilities, and you should think carefully before acting. The most obvious choice is the police. They will probably regard it as their duty to check your story; but in most countries, with the exception of France and the USA, where certain official procedures exist, there will be little they can actually do.

CORROBORATION

In some cases, the police may refer the matter to the Defence Ministry. But, as often as not, the sighting will get no further than your local police station. Unfortunately, this is inevitable. The police have many tasks to perform and experience has taught them that most UFO reports are not really very important. Consequently, they tend to be given a low priority. But the police should certainly be contacted if you think that the object you have seen has landed. Their presence at the scene of the landing would provide very valuable corroboration. Otherwise, it is probably advisable not to waste their time.

Another agency you may think of notifying is the local airfield, either civil or military. As with the police, there is generally little they can do, or are prepared to do, unless it seems to them that your report justifies calling in a defence establishment. Airport staff may be able to tell you if any aircraft were in the area at the time of your sighting, but it is not advisable to ask them if they have read anything unusual on their radar. A denial might mean that they genuinely had not, or it could be that they had, but for some reason were not willing to tell you. The matter, for example, might already have been passed on to the Defence Ministry, who would want to make their own investigations.

As far as newspapers, radio and television are concerned, try to resist the temptation to approach them. The media will probably be interested only if they think they can use your story, and that may depend on whether it is quiet or busy in the newsroom, rather than on the credibility or intrinsic interest of your sighting.

SCIENTIFIC APPRAISAL

The most sensible step to take if you have seen what you believe to be a UFO is to contact a UFO investigator as soon as possible. They are trained to help you and to record accurately the necessary information for scientific appraisal.

There are many kinds of UFO investigator and UFO investigation group. Some are motivated by an almost religious belief in UFOs and will be biased. Others may border on the eccentric, attracting cranks and frauds. Most, however, are serious-minded and will be concerned with establishing the authenticity of your sighting. A list of reputable UFO organisations and their addresses is given at the end of this article. If your country is not included in

*In*Focus

TEST YOUR POWERS OF OBSERVATION

When witnessing any strange or dramatic event, such as spotting a UFO, it is very important to be able to recall exactly what you saw. But try this experiment: look at the picture on the left for about 10 seconds. Now stop reading this article, while you try to remember what was in the picture. Draw it from memory. You will probably find that your attempt is far from being a perfect reproduction of the original.

You might think this experiment has little relevance to UFO spotting. Surely a UFO would present such an unusual sight that it would make an indelible impression on the memory? Experience with witnesses of accidents or crimes, which are not everyday observations for most people, does not bear this out. What we see is not always the same as what we are able to recall having seen.

After looking at the picture, men will probably be more likely to have recall of the attractive young woman walking along the street. Women, on the other hand, are more likely to remember details of her clothing.

Our memories of what we have seen tend to be conditioned by what interests us personally. And what we remember also depends to some extent on past experiences – what we are used to seeing. People unfamiliar with the type of lamp post in this street will probably have noticed one in the picture, but may not remember certain other details. Similarly, there will be some who fail to spot the UFO on first glancing at the picture, or even after staring at it for a while. How much did *you* take in?

---

the list, it does not necessarily mean that there is no serious UFO society there. Write to the British address. All the groups listed are associated with the international UFO magazine *Flying Saucer Review*, which is distributed in over 60 countries. Your letter will be forwarded to a local agency.

Each report is treated confidentially and almost all UFO groups use a standard report form. You will probably be asked to fill in one of these forms. You might also be asked if it is possible for a UFO investigator to come and see you at a time and place of your choosing.

Naturally, if you happen to come face to face with what you may think is a UFO, it is not always easy to remember exactly what to do. The oddness of the occasion may well lead you to panic. Yet it is always worth trying to remain calm and remembering the procedures outlined in this article. The more well-authenticated, well-documented, cases there are, the more will eventually be discovered about these elusive intruders.

UFO ORGANISATIONS

IF YOU ARE CONVINCED YOU HAVE SEEN A UFO, YOU MAY LIKE TO SEND YOUR OUTLINE REPORT TO ONE OF THE FOLLOWING BODIES. DETAILED FORMS ARE AVAILABLE FOR RECORDING EVERY ASPECT OF SUCH SIGHTINGS.

UK
British UFO Research Association
16 Southway
Burgess Hill
Sussex RH15 9ST

Flying Saucer Review
PO Box 162
High Wycombe
Bucks HP13 5DZ

GERMANY
Journal für UFO-Forschung
Postfach 2361
D-5880 Lüdenscheid 1
Germany

NORTH AMERICA
MUFON
103 Oldtowne Road
Seguin
Texas 78155
USA

AUSTRALASIA
ACUFOS
Box 728
Lane Cove
NSW 2066
Australia

The photograph, *left,* is one of the few shots of a nocturnal UFO to show more than an indeterminate blur of light. It was taken by a 14-year-old paper-boy in Tulsa, Oklahoma, USA, on 2 August 1965. The object was observed by many witnesses, who stated that the tricoloured lights changed slowly to a uniform blue-green. The Condon Committee, set up at the University of Colorado, confirmed that the photograph represented a large object seen against the sky, and that the dark stripes between the bright patches were neither space nor sky, but part of the UFO itself. With characteristic caution, the US Air Force concluded that the photograph represented either a genuine UFO or a Christmas tree light! The UFO organisation Ground Saucer Watch, on the other hand, considers it strong UFO evidence.

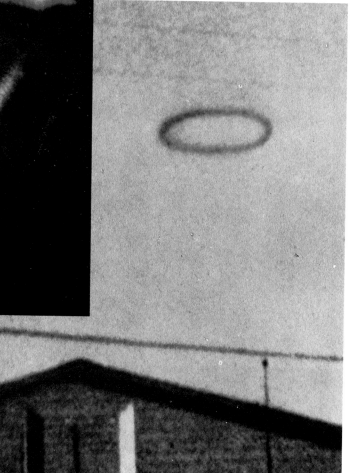

At about 9.00 a.m. one day in September 1957, the strange, ring-shaped object, *right,* was seen in the sky over Fort Belvoir, Virginia, USA. It 'seemed solid', very black with no reflection and was about 60 feet (18 metres) in diameter. The ring gradually became engulfed in black smoke and finally disappeared. The Condon Committee later identified the sighting, however, as having been 'an atomic bomb simulation demonstration of the type commonly carried out at Fort Belvoir at this period'.

The still, *left,* is from a film taken by Ralph Mayher in Miami, Florida, USA on 29 July 1952. Using computer techniques to analyse the photograph, the American UFO organisation Ground Saucer Watch has established that it is probably genuine and that it shows an object 30-40 feet (9-12 metres) long. Mayher reported that its speed appeared to be less than that of a falling meteorite as it shot away over the ocean.

Puzzled by his sighting, Mayher turned his film over to the US Air Force for investigation. It was never returned. Many people see the incident as part of a deliberate campaign on the part of the US authorities to suppress evidence of UFOs. Luckily, Mayher had foreseen the possibility of his film getting 'lost': so before handing it over, he carefully snipped off the first few frames. This is one of them.

The photograph of an alleged flying saucer over Venezuela, *above,* is in fact a hoax by an engineer in Caracas. He placed a photograph of a button on an enlargement of an aerial shot, which was then rephotographed; and the 'saucer's' shadow was 'burned' in at the printing stage.

The photograph, *right,* confirmed as probably genuine by Ground Saucer Watch, was taken early in the afternoon of 8 May 1966 by James Pfeiffer, an airline executive on holiday in Ipameri, Brazil. The object was seen by a couple of dozen witnesses. GSW's computer analysis of the photograph shows that the object was approximately 450 yards (400 metres) from the camera at an altitude of about 160-230 feet (50-70 metres). The witnesses heard a 'high-, then a low-pitched whining sound' as the object crossed the river. It brushed against trees as it disappeared from view; and broken branches were found in the area later. The entire sighting lasted about 90 seconds.

many different types of lighting, there are plenty of opportunities for strange effects. Bright searchlights, used in front of the plane, may be visible from miles away. Seen heading towards you, such lights can appear stationary for a long time before bursting into colour as the aircraft's navigation lights come into view. In many countries, aircraft are also employed for advertising by using electronic lights that flash out a computer-programmed message. The aircraft is built to fly very slowly so that the message can be read. But if the lights are seen from an angle, it is common for very weird effects to result.

Aircraft are, of course, highly manoeuvrable, – helicopters even more so. Consequently, not only might they be seen as lights on a smooth flightpath, but can also be seen to alter direction, slow down, and even stop in mid-flight. The wind, meanwhile, can carry away the sound of an aircraft's engines, leaving only a silent light in the sky.

Most of these effects would be seen only at night. But there is one object that is often seen and

you know where to look. But often there are good reasons why stars and planets are not immediately recognised for what they are. Optical illusion, for example, and the phenomenon known as *autokinesis*, which causes a star apparently to dart about erratically in the sky, are common causes of misidentification. Since stars do not normally dart about, this effect instills the belief that the light comes not from a star but from a UFO.

FLIGHTPATHS

If the light does appear to move, the next question is whether it follows a smooth flightpath or whether it hovers or seems to change direction dramatically. A smooth flightpath can indicate one of several things. Precisely what it is can usually be determined by the length of time for which the light is seen. If it is of very short duration, for instance, it could be a meteor – particles of dust or debris from space burning up as they enter the Earth's atmosphere. Meteors tend to glow for a second or two, leaving a trail of light.

// TO HELP WITNESSES DISTINGUISH BETWEEN WHAT IS AND WHAT IS NOT A UFO, THE TERM 'TRUE UFO' IS USED FOR SOMETHING THAT DOES NOT APPEAR, AFTER INVESTIGATION, TO BE A CASE OF MISTAKEN IDENTITY. //

Occasionally, the debris is a little larger than usual and takes longer to burn up. This leads to the phenomenon known as a *bolide* or fireball, a brilliant light visible for up to 10 seconds and accompanied by a rumbling or whooshing sound. Fireballs have been seen in daylight too, although this is fairly rare. Usually, sightings of fireballs are so spectacular that

It is not easy to recognise the irregular, unearthly shape silhouetted against the sun, above left, as a flight of helicopters.

The spectacular comet Ikeya-Seki, left, was seen in late 1965. Like a surprising number of heavenly bodies – including stars and planets – it was reported as a UFO.

they are witnessed by dozens of people over a wide area. But on the whole they are very similar in appearance to a satellite re-entry, which is another common cause of UFO misidentification.

Circling the Earth are hundreds of man-made satellites. Many are too small to be seen from the ground, but others are visible at night as points of light that may take several minutes to cross the sky. When they re-enter the Earth's atmosphere, they can present a spectacular sight. As the pieces burn away, they glow in several colours, leaving a trail through the upper atmosphere, which can take several minutes to disappear. A few parts may even survive and reach the ground, as happened to the American Skylab, for example, which landed in Western Australia in July 1979.

But by far the most common causes of UFO misidentification are aircraft. Since aircraft possess

the irregular shape of its body could easily be taken to be a UFO.

In most cases, the object believed to be a UFO is seen moving in a constant direction at varying speeds. In strong sunlight, for example, an aeroplane's wings and tailplane can be obscured, leaving just a metallic body or cylinder visible. Though really the fuselage, it can look just like a UFO. Even clouds have been mistaken for UFOs. One type, for example – a lenticular formation – looks like a structured disc. Though uncommon, its slow movement has certainly fooled more than one observer.

Flocks of birds have also caused confusion. In daylight, the reflective underbellies of certain species can shine in sunlight and may be seen as white ovals, obscuring all other detail. At night, it is even possible for street lighting to be reflected, creating different coloured oval shapes, according to the type of lighting used.

Clearly, there are many possible causes of misidentification. What Captain Mantell encountered over Kentucky, for instance, was probably one

The rare lenticular cloud formation, top, has the characteristic shape of a 'flying saucer'.

Objects such as the high-flying kite, above, glinting in the sunlight with its control wires invisible, can also take on the appearance of a typical UFO. The research balloon, right, was sent up 130,000 feet (40,000 metres) to investigate cosmic rays. Even experienced airmen have failed to recognise craft like this for what they are.

misidentified as a UFO during the day – the balloon. Weather centres release balloons at regular intervals, either to test wind direction or to carry instruments high into the sky from where they radio meteorological information back to Earth. At a high altitude, a balloon will reflect sunlight from its shiny surface while floating across the sky; and from the ground, the silvery dot, drifting across the sky, may be seen as a round or conical shape.

> **THE BELGIAN AIR FORCE HAS BEEN ON ALERT FOR THREE NIGHTS RUNNING .... SEVERAL TIMES THE UFO WAS SEEN FROM THE GROUND, BUT EACH TIME THE AIRCRAFT GOT THERE TOO LATE. [IT] TENDED TO HOVER JUST ABOVE THE ROOFTOPS, TOO LOW TO BE CONFRONTED BY AN AIRCRAFT.**
>
> THE FINANCIAL TIMES, 1990

Medium-definition experiences are those that involve the clear perception of a shape. Though they have sometimes been seen at night, they are more commonly seen in daytime. They account for a further 35 per cent of all UFO cases and, as with low-definition experiences, the most important criterion is motion. A clearly defined shape that hovers for some time is unlikely to be an aircraft, although it could be a helicopter, too distant to be heard.

Airships tend also to be a common cause of misidentification. Under certain conditions, their shape could be mistaken for a cigar-shaped UFO, hovering or moving slowly across the sky. Kites are another possible explanation. Seen at a distance, the controlling cord of a kite may not be visible, and

of the 100-foot (30.5-metre) 'skyhook' balloons, which were secretly being tested in the area at the time by the US Navy. These balloons were not known to Air Force officers; and although this was the probable identity of Mantell's UFO, the case has never been conclusively proven. The 'official' explanation that what observers on the ground saw was the planet Venus is definitely not convincing to the majority of investigators.

As for the case of the Hertfordshire policemen, it was subsequently discovered that a Russian booster-rocket had re-entered the Earth's atmosphere that night. As it happened, its orbit took it over northern Europe, and it was this that many witnesses probably mistook for a UFO. The New Zealand film was not connected to the Hertfordshire incident at all. But there are still those who remain convinced that what the two policemen had seen was a true UFO.

The photograph, **above,** was taken by a coastguard, R. Alpert, at 9.35 a.m. on 16 July 1952 from the control tower at Salem Air Base in Massachusetts, USA. The objects were reported to be moving at great speed; but they appear much brighter in the photograph than they actually were because the aperture of the camera was set for the brightness of the surrounding landscape. Consequently, the UFOs themselves are over-exposed.

But is the photography genuine? The images are unlikely to have been caused by lens flares, as these almost always appear in straight lines. But it is reported that the picture was taken through a laboratory window; and sceptics have suggested that the objects could actually be reflections of lights inside the laboratory. Photographic experts, however, point out that reflected lights are rarely as opaque as these.

The picture, **right,** was taken by London photographer Anwar Hussein in the Spanish Pyrenees in July 1978. After finishing filming one day, he found he had left one of his lenses at the top of a mountain. The next morning, at about 9 o'clock, he returned to look for it. He found the lens and took some pictures, his camera set on motor-drive. At the time, he noticed nothing unusual except the brightness of the light and the uncanny quietness. Back in London, he sent the film to be developed, and later received a worried telephone call from the lab, who pointed out the 'object' on the film and thought it must be a fault that had appeared during developing. On examination, however, the emulsion was found to be undamaged. This is typical of many of the best UFO pictures, which are often of objects that go unnoticed at the time of filming but which show up later on the negatives.

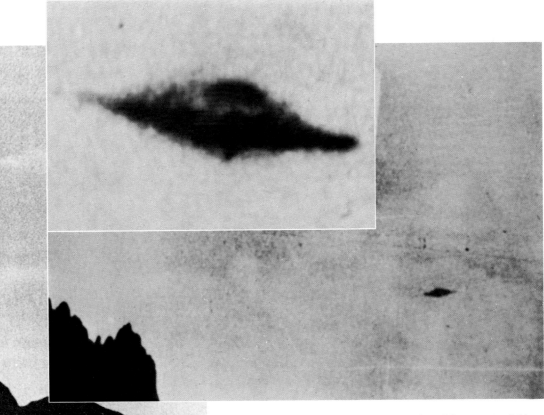

Early in January 1958, a survey ship of the Brazilian Navy, the Almirante Saldanha, set off from Rio de Janeiro, bound for the rocky island of Trindade, where the Navy had an oceanographic station. Among those on board was Almiro Barauna, a specialist in underwater photography.

Just before the ship was due to set sail on the return journey at 12.15 p.m. on 16 January 1958, a retired Air Force officer, Captain Viegas, who was on deck with other officers and technicians, called to Barauna that there was a bright object in the sky. Barauna located it and watched the moving object until it was silhouetted against some cloud. Then he shot the two photographs, **above.** The UFO disappeared behind the main peak of the island for a few seconds. When it reappeared, it was flying in the opposite direction. Barauna took a third photograph, then a fourth and fifth, but these last two were wasted shots because the photographer was jostled by the other people aboard the ship, who were by now extremely excited about what they were witnessing. The UFO appeared briefly to halt its passage away from the island, and Barauna took his last picture of the object as it moved swiftly away.

The photographer said the object was silent, dark grey in colour, and apparently surrounded by a greenish vapour or mist.

Barauna developed his film on board ship in the presence of the skipper, Commander Bacellar. (As there was no photographic paper on board, prints were made once the ship had returned to Rio.) Barauna said that, in the urgency and excitement of the sighting, he had not thought to check the settings of his camera and the pictures were consequently over-exposed.

Back in Rio de Janeiro, the Brazilian Navy examined the negatives. They found them to be genuine, and any possibility of a hoax was eliminated. Based on Barauna's account, the naval authorities then set up a mock re-run of the incident, and were able to compute the speed of the object as about 550-600 mph (900-1000 km/h). The diameter of the Saturn-shaped UFO was estimated at around 40 yards (37 metres). At least 100 people had seen the UFO, and the photographs seem to be unimpeachable.

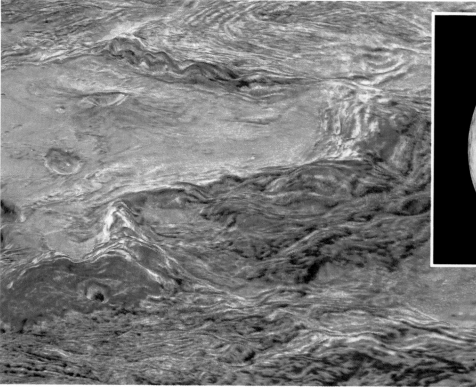

The planet Venus, above, is some 26 million miles (48 million kilometres) from Earth. With a surface temperature reaching 900°F (480°C), it is virtually impossible that anything could live on Venus, shown left in an artist's impression.

SPINNING THROUGH SPACE

REPORTS OF UFOS DESCRIBE DISC-SHAPED, HIGHLY MANOEUVRABLE, IMMENSELY FAST-FLYING MACHINES, CAPABLE OF FEATS THAT DEFY ALL KNOWN PHYSICAL LAWS. WHAT KIND OF CIVILISATIONS MIGHT HAVE PRODUCED THEM?

Apollo 8 blasts off for the Moon, below. To reach planets beyond our solar system, however, would require a spacecraft powered by a vastly more efficient fuel.

The term UFO – unidentified flying object – officially means simply something that has not been, or cannot be, accounted for by any of the known laws of physics. But the seemingly rational behaviour reported in many UFO sightings, as well as the accounts of meetings with humanoids, have led to frequent speculation that UFOs are, in fact, spacecraft bringing creatures from outer space to Earth.

If this is so, the spaceships must be able to cover immense distances. Indeed, people who claim to have had contact with extra-terrestrials often say they have spoken with Venusians. Yet Venus is highly unlikely to be inhabited. So any intelligent life forms must be coming from still further away; and, even assuming that lifespans of creatures from other planets may be much longer than our own, it is clear that UFOs must be able to travel very fast indeed if they are not to take hundreds of years to travel between inhabited planets.

Reports of the movement of UFOs are also remarkably consistent. Most people describe them as hovering and then taking off at very high speed, often executing manoeuvres that would be impossible in conventional aircraft. Even allowing for exaggeration, the consistency of reports suggests that UFOs must be using a very powerful force indeed to produce such dramatic accelerations.

None of the rocket fuels we use at present can produce either the speed or acceleration observed in UFOs, because they store only a small amount of energy for a given mass. Right from the beginning, space travel has been faced with the problem of enabling rockets to carry enough fuel for a journey – they must lift the fuel, which can be very heavy if the journey is long, as well as themselves and their occupants. The solution has been the multi-stage rocket: initial acceleration is given by a rocket that is jettisoned when its fuel is used up and a second rocket takes over.

Although our rockets eventually reach quite high speeds, they are nowhere near fast enough to reach planets outside our solar system within a

Professor Freeman Dyson, above, is the American physicist who designed a nuclear-powered spacecraft as long ago as 1958.

human lifetime. If we assume UFOs are subject to the same laws of physics as we are, in order to operate on and near the Earth with the rapid accelerations and manoeuvres at high speeds that are often reported, they must be using a different source of energy from conventional chemical fuels. Indeed, their fuel must be highly compact, with a high energy yield for a small mass, for which the obvious source is nuclear.

As long ago as 1958 – just after the Russians launched the first man-made satellites into space – a brilliant theoretical physicist called Freeman Dyson embarked on a plan for a nuclear-powered spaceship. He had previously worked on the development of the atom bomb and had a comprehensive understanding of nuclear power. Assembling a group of scientists at La Jolla, in southern California, to work with him, he now embarked upon 'Project Orion' – a serious attempt to build a spacecraft powered by nuclear explosions.

PROJECT ORION

Freeman Dyson's ultimate aim was to build a spacecraft the size of a small city that would take a group of people to a distant comet on the edge of the solar system, where they would settle. This may have been a pipe-dream, but the design was real enough.

The spacecraft was to be powered by hydrogen bombs. Essentially, his idea was to carry a number of hydrogen bombs aboard the spacecraft: these would be moved, one by one, to a position underneath the craft where they would be exploded. The base of the spacecraft would absorb the shock, and the craft would be driven along. Obviously, the bomb system would have to be designed so that the craft was propelled and not simply blown apart; but – in principle, at least – this was staightforward. However, Dyson was never able to test his ideas: he was prevented by public concern about pollution of the atmosphere by radioactive fallout.

UFOs are often reported as disappearing rapidly – going off 'like a television set' and reappearing just as quickly. This aspect of the phenomenon has puzzled scientists for a long time and has led to suggestions that UFOs use some kind of 'anti-optic device' to prevent them being seen. There are, however, some simpler explanations that could account for the majority of reports. UFOs 'disappearing' in the darkness of night could do so by simply switching off their lights; and daytime discs could appear to vanish by turning themselves sideways on to the observer. (It would be difficult to pick out the thin edge of a disc against the sky.) These explanations do not, of course, account for radar-visual sightings that suddenly vanish. But if a UFO disappeared behind a patch of disturbed air, a mirage-like effect could easily screen it both from sight and from radar detectors.

There are, however, cases on file for which none of these explanations is credible. Indeed, it seems that the phenomena involved can only be explained as products of a technology much further advanced than our own.

PERSPECTIVES

WHY SAUCERS?

By far the majority of UFO reports describe the objects seen as disc or cigar-shaped; and it could even be that most UFOs reported as cigar-shaped are in fact discs. Whether or not this is actually the case, the number of reports of saucer-shaped UFOs is overwhelming. There has also been a great deal of speculation as to why this should be so, some people suggesting that the mystical significance of the circle may have something to do with it. But there could be a simpler explanation.

On long inter-stellar voyages, a spacecraft will pass through vast regions of empty space - far from the regions of gravitational attraction of any major objects - where there is no wind resistance, no 'up' or 'down', no east or west, nothing. The most logical shape for a vessel travelling in these circumstances is circular, for a circle is symmetrical about an infinite number of axes. The fact that most UFOs are disc-shaped rather than spherical can be explained as a design feature that allows spacecraft to operate at high speeds once they have entered the atmosphere of planets. By flying with their edges into the wind, they can - in theory, at least - cut down the effect of air resistance almost to zero.

SILENTLY, OUT OF THE NIGHT SKY

SCIENTISTS GENERALLY CONSIDER UFOs THAT GIVE RESPONSES ON RADAR SCOPES THE MOST RELIABLE FOR THEIR PURPOSES. THE SIGHTING DESCRIBED BELOW TOOK PLACE AT CASELLE AIRPORT IN TURIN, ITALY, AND IS ONE OF THE MOST WELL DOCUMENTED RADAR-VISUAL SIGHTINGS ON RECORD

I n all, it lasted for five months in the winter of 1973 to 1974. It was heralded by a first impressive sighting at Turin in November 1973 – an event of profound significance for the science of ufology that attracted the attention of Jean-Claude Bourret, a top reporter from the French radio station *France-Inter,* who broadcast a series of programmes about UFOs, culminating in a startling and important interview with the then Minister of Defence, Robert Galley.

On 30 November 1973, Riccardo Marano was preparing to land his Piper Navajo at Caselle Airport when he was advised by control that there was an unidentified object at a height of about 4,000 feet (1,200 metres) above the runway, close to where he was due to land. Control had the object on its radar screens and gave Marano permission to approach it to see what it was. As he neared his target, control reported that it was heading for the Susa Valley. Accordingly, Marano changed course to follow it, when suddenly control announced that the target had disappeared from its radar.

At that moment, Marano received a message from another aircraft; the UFO was behind him at about 12,000 feet (3,600 metres). Marano's Navajo was then flying at about 10,000 feet (3,000 metres). He began to turn, and saw in front of him what

appeared to be a bright, white luminous sphere, which was emitting light of all colours of the spectrum. The light pulsated from bright to dim, but never went out completely. As he approached the UFO, Marano reported that it was 'flying in a most irregular fashion, making fantastic lateral deviations and sudden vast jumps to and fro'. Taking advantage of a moment when the object was below him, Marano put his plane into a dive, accelerating to a speed of over 250 mph (400 km/h), but he could not catch up with the UFO. When he abandoned the chase, it was heading south-eastwards. He estimated its speed at about 550 mph (900 km/h).

SIGHTING CONFIRMED

Two other pilots confirmed the presence of the object. They were Comandante Tranquillo, who had just taken off in his Alitalia DC-9, and Comandante Mezzalani, who was bringing in his Alitalia DC-9 from Paris. Comandante Tranquillo advised control that he dared not approach the 'shining object giving out flashes' and thereupon adjusted his course.

Comandante Mezzalani observed the object as he was touching down. He said it was large and bright, yet somehow dimmer than a star or an artificial satellite.

There was another very reliable witness, too – none other than the commander of the neighbouring Caselle military airfie!d, Colonello Rustichelli, who stated that he had observed the UFO on his radar screen. It was, he said, something solid, which lit up like an aircraft on his radar screen, giving the

The artist's impressions, below and opposite, show the luminous spheres witnessed at Caselle Airport, Turin in 1973 from the aircraft, above right.

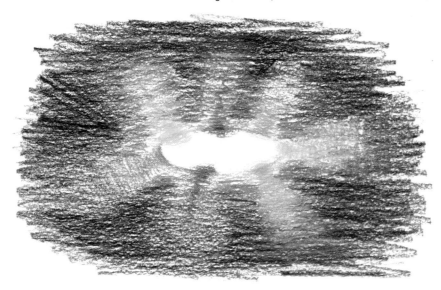

COMANDANTE TRANQUILLO ADVISED CONTROL THAT HE DARED NOT APPROACH THE SHINING OBJECT GIVING OUT FLASHES AND THEREUPON ADJUSTED HIS COURSE.

The other person whose interest was aroused by the Turin incident was Robert Galley, Minister of Defence for France, who granted an exclusive interview to Bourret, broadcast to the nation on 21 February 1974.

SECRET SECTION

This interview was of immense importance for the science of ufology. In it, the serving Minister of Defence admitted not only that UFOs exist, but also that in 1954 his government had set up a secret section devoted to their study. Galley spoke of the massive nature of the UFO phenomena, of the many detailed eyewitness reports he had read, and of the volume of reports received from the Air Force in the early days of the project. Since 1970, UFO research in France has been in the hands of the *Centre Nationale d'Etudes Spatiales* (The National Centre for Space Studies), which evaluates reports of UFO sightings from both the Air Force and the Gendarmerie. Unfortunately, however, the French UFO group has no contact with international military groups.

This startling interview was immediately given wide coverage in the French papers, including *France-Soir, Le Parisien Libéré, L'Aurore* and *Le Figaro*, as well as all the big provincial papers. It was soon reported in German, Spanish, Swiss, Italian, Brazilian and American newspapers, too, but not in the British press, nor on radio or television. In his English translation of Jean-Claude Bourret's book *The Crack in the Universe*, Gordon Creighton describes his unsuccessful attempts to convince the BBC that the interview was important enough to warrant a mention on one of its radio science programmes. He even suggests that the scant and biased reporting of the UFO phenomena by the British media may be the result of an official debunking attitude on the part of the authorities. Their methods are certainly different from those used in the USA.

Indeed, Creighton says: 'Quieter and more subtle techniques of ridicule and denigration plus, no doubt, the occasional discreet telephone call to the newspaper that has offended by printing a serious looking UFO report, have yielded far better results than the CIA's methods.'

This scepticism on the part of the authorities no doubt accounts for the fact that very little serious scientific research is carried out into UFOs in Britain. Amateur UFO societies can do little more than monitor sightings. Suppression of information can only be harmful to research, and it is disturbing to think there may be many UFO sightings we simply never hear about.

same sort of return as a DC-9. He said that it had looked like a star; but when he got it on his radar, it stayed firm. Soon afterwards, it had headed off westwards.

A curious event, which may be connected with the UFO sightings described above, had taken place earlier on the same evening. At 5.00 p.m., Franco Contin, an amateur photographer, saw an extremely bright object in the sky. At first he thought it was a star; but when he saw it begin to move about, he realised it must be something else. A slightly misshapen luminous globe, it was white at first and then suddenly turned deep orange. Contin fetched his camera and took a total of eight photographs. These show an enormous object, oval in shape and brightly luminous.

RADIO COVERAGE

The Turin sighting was remarkable not only because it was followed by a world-wide wave of UFO reports, but also because it attracted the attention of two very important people. The first of these was Jean-Claude Bourret, chief reporter of the radio station *France-Inter,* who was so impressed by the report of the sighting that he made a series of 39 radio programmes entirely devoted to UFO research, which were broadcast between January 1973 and March 1974.

Robert Galley, then French Minister of Defence, is seen below in his historic interview with reporter Jean-Claude Bourret of the French radio station France-Inter on 21 February 1974. Galley admitted that the French government had been secretly studying UFOs for 20 years.

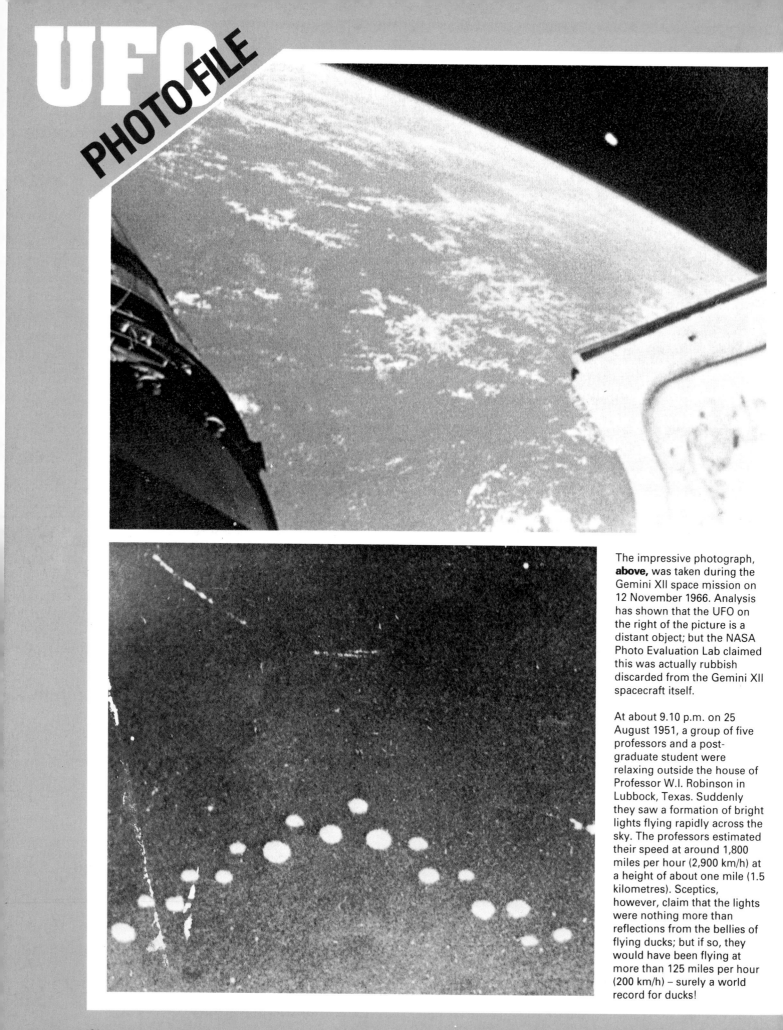

The impressive photograph, **above,** was taken during the Gemini XII space mission on 12 November 1966. Analysis has shown that the UFO on the right of the picture is a distant object; but the NASA Photo Evaluation Lab claimed this was actually rubbish discarded from the Gemini XII spacecraft itself.

At about 9.10 p.m. on 25 August 1951, a group of five professors and a post-graduate student were relaxing outside the house of Professor W.I. Robinson in Lubbock, Texas. Suddenly they saw a formation of bright lights flying rapidly across the sky. The professors estimated their speed at around 1,800 miles per hour (2,900 km/h) at a height of about one mile (1.5 kilometres). Sceptics, however, claim that the lights were nothing more than reflections from the bellies of flying ducks; but if so, they would have been flying at more than 125 miles per hour (200 km/h) – surely a world record for ducks!

The UFO **below** was observed by three witnesses near Saas Fee, Switzerland, on 26 July 1975. It seemed to be metallic and was difficult to make out against the mountain fog. It was also reported to be humming softly.

The photograph has been rigorously analysed by the American UFO organisation Ground Saucer Watch of Phoenix, Arizona. The techniques they use can reveal a number of details not immediately apparent from a photograph, including the time, to within an hour, at which the shot was taken, the apparent size of the UFO, its distance from the camera, and any supporting threads or structures that may indicate a hoax.

The black-and-white picture, **right,** shows a computer digital image enhancement of the original. It passed the test.

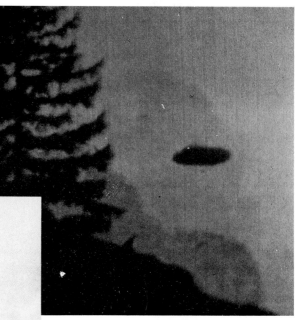

The photograph, **below,** also passed GSW's computer test. It was taken by Deputy Sheriff Strauch while on a hunting trip in Gibbon, Minnesota, USA on 21 October 1965. It shows a typical UFO – a bright, blurred, disc-shaped light – and illustrates the difficulty of taking accurate colour pictures of UFOs in poor light conditions. The strange colour of the sky makes it possible to deduce that the original object was probably a shade of red, another feature that links it with other UFO sightings.

THE BRITISH SCARESHIP INVASION

A POLICEMAN'S SIGHTING OF A HUGE AND MYSTERIOUS AIRSHIP EARLY IN 1909 STARTED A SPATE OF REPORTS OF SIMILAR TERRIFYING CRAFT. WERE THEY GERMAN ZEPPELINS – OR PERHAPS SOMETHING MUCH STRANGER?

In the early months of 1909, an aerial horror began to haunt the imaginations of the British people. The first sighting of a phantom airship to have a major impact on the public consciousness was made by a Cambridgeshire policeman, PC Kettle. He was patrolling Cromwell Road in Peterborough on the morning of 23 March when he heard the sound of a distant motor car. As he continued to hear what he thought was the steady buzz of a high-power engine, he suddenly realised that the noise was coming from above. On looking up, he saw a bright light attached to a long, oblong body outlined against the stars. This strange aerial object crossed the sky at a high speed, and was soon lost from sight.

News of this sighting met with a certain amount of scepticism. Nevertheless, it set the pattern for future 'airship' watchers, and reports from people

An early dirigible, the Zeppelin Mark 2, is seen above in flight over Lake Constance in April 1909. The same year, there was a spate of mystery airship sightings throughout Britain. Many people believed that the aircraft were German Zeppelins making reconnaissance flights in preparation for an invasion of Britain – but German airships were far too unreliable for it to be possible to employ them on such a dangerous mission.

It was at Cromwell Road, Peterborough, below, that the first 'scareship' sighting occurred.

who had seen bright, powerful lamps or searchlights attached to dark bodies making a noisy passage across the night sky soon became numerous. Another common feature of such stories was the happy habit of many self-proclaimed experts of submitting explanations for such visions. In the case of PC Kettle's sighting, a Peterborough police officer announced to the press that a 'very fine kite flying over the neighbourhood of Cobden Street' had been the cause. The bright light was easily explained as a Chinese lantern that had been attached to the kite.

'But how about the matter of the airship going at a tremendous pace?' asked a reporter.

'Oh, that was a little poetic touch on Kettle's part for the benefit of you interviewers. He did not officially report that, and the wind driving the kite would give the impression of movement,' replied the officer.

'But how do you get over the whirring and beating of engines?' asked the still puzzled reporter.

'Oh, that,' responded the officer, as he went to take his leave, 'was the the motor which goes all night in the Co-operative Bakery in Cobden Street!'

This dismissal of PC Kettle's observation might have carried more weight if it had been released soon after the sighting. Instead, it took the police at least six weeks to arrive at this simple answer to the mystery of the airship. It seems they preferred to imply that PC Kettle was a simpleton who could not distinguish between a kite and an airship, rather than to see the Peterborough police force implicated in giving credence to such an unlikely story.

A clipping from the **Cardiff Evening Express and Evening Mail** *of Wednesday, 19 May 1909, right, describes a sighting of the mystery airship made on 18 May on Caerphilly Mountain. The witness saw a huge 'long, tube-shaped object' lying on the grass at the side of the road. Newspaper cuttings relating to airship sightings and to German military matters were later found scattered over the area.*

At first, PC Kettle's observation seemed to have been an isolated occurrence. But around the beginning of May, sightings began to be reported daily throughout south-east England. A typical report was made by a certain C. W. Allen. As he and some friends were driving through the village of Kelmarsh, Northamptonshire, they suddenly heard a loud bang. Then, above them, they heard the 'tock-tock-tock' of a motor engine. Although the sky was dark, they were able to see a 100-foot (30-metre) long, torpedo-shaped airship that carried lights fore and aft. It was moving swiftly, but this did not prevent the witnesses seeing a platform beneath the craft, which appeared to contain its crew. The airship then disappeared in the direction of Peterborough.

Prior to the First World War, Britain devoted very little research to airships, such as the Wellman, below, seen at the Aero Show of 1909. Government construction was begun in 1907; but by the outbreak of war in 1914, only five British ships had been built.

There were many more such reports. But what were these craft? The fact that the exploits of Count Zeppelin were well-known in Britain, combined with the antagonism between Germany and Britain at the time, soon led people to the conclusion that German airships were probably making a reconnaissance of southern England.

The major flaw in this hypothesis, however, was the sheer number of airship sighting reports, which soon came from all regions of Britain. At the time, Germany barely had the resources to make even one or two reconnaissance flights. For this reason, a few newspapers were prepared to discount the entire phenomenon as imaginary, and sent readers who had reported airship sightings to what they picturesquely called 'lunacy experts'. From one, they received this diagnosis:

'In every thousand men, there are always two every night who see strange matters – chromatic rats, luminous owls, moving lights, fiery comets and things like these. So you can always get plenty

A PHANTOM FLEET?

Could the mysterious airships seen over Britain during 1909 have been German Zeppelins? It seems unlikely.
The pioneer of German airship research was Count Ferdinand von Zeppelin, *right*, who launched his first dirigible, the *Luftschiff Zeppelin 1* – or LZ1 – over Lake Constance in July 1900, shortly before his sixty-second birthday. LZ1, simply an enormous bag filled with gas and propelled by an engine, remained in the air for just over 17 minutes – but its short flight was impressive, and the future of airships seemed bright.

Count Zeppelin set in motion an ambitious airship-building programme; but by 1909, owing to a number of crashes and shortage of money, there were only three working Zeppelins in existence – the LZ3, rebuilt from an earlier airship that had crashed, the LZ5 and the LZ6. Of these, only two, the LZ3 and the LZ5, were in the hands of the German army. They were very much in their experimental stages, and certainly not capable of long and hazardous journeys, or of carrying out high-speed manoeuvres, such as those reported by the numerous witnesses of the British 'scareships'.

of evidence of this sort, particularly when you suggest it to the patient first.'

The most puzzling and sensational sighting was made by an elderly Punch and Judy showman, C. Lethbridge. With this report, made on 18 May, the focus for the airship's activities shifted from the east coast to mid-Glamorgan, Wales. By now, there were also well-attested reports of a 'long-shaped object' with red flashing lights seen over Belfast, now in Northern Ireland, on 17 May, and there seemed to be no area of Britain left unaffected by the scare. A few hours after his sighting which amounted to a close encounter, Lethbridge told reporters:

'Yesterday, I went to Senghenydd and proceeded to walk home over Caerphilly Mountain. You know that the top of the mountain is a very lonely spot. I reached it about 11 p.m. and, when turning the bend at the summit, I was surprised to see a

long, tube-shaped affair lying on the grass at the roadside, with two men busily engaged with something nearby. They attracted my close attention because of their peculiar get-up: they appeared to have big, heavy fur coats and fur caps fitting tightly over their heads. I was rather frightened, but I continued to go on until I was within twenty yards [18 metres] of them and then my idea as to their clothing was confirmed. The noise of my little spring-cart seemed to attract them and, when they saw me, they jumped up and jabbered furiously to each other in a strange lingo – Welsh or something else; it was certainly not English. They hurriedly collected something from the ground, and then I was really frightened. The long thing on the ground rose up slowly. I was standing still all the time, quite amazed; and when it was hanging a few feet off the ground, the men jumped into a kind of little carriage

As depicted left, the 'scareship' seen on Caerphilly Mountain on 18 May 1909 'rose in the air in a zig-zag fashion' and sailed away towards Cardiff.

At Ham Common, on the outskirts of London, right, *on the night of 13 May 1909, two witnesses saw a remarkable airship. The pilots, described as a Yankee and a German, apparently steered their craft by pulling beer handles.*

suspended from it, and gradually the whole affair and the men rose in the air in a zig-zag fashion. When they had cleared the telegraph wires that pass over the mountain, two lights like electric lamps shone out, and the thing went higher into the air and sailed away towards Cardiff.'

When Lethbridge, accompanied by reporters, returned to the site where he had his encounter, they found several traces of the airship's presence. The ground where the 45-foot (14-metre) long object had been seen was churned up as though by a plough-share. All over the area, they discovered a quantity of newspaper cuttings of accounts of airship sightings and references to the German emperor and army. Along with these items, they found a large quantity of papier-mâché packing material, a lid from a tin of metal polish, a few dozen pieces of blue paper bearing strange writing, and a metal pin with a red label attached to it. The label of the pin carried instructions in French and excited attention when some commentators thought that it was part of an explosive device, but further enquiry showed it probably to have been a valve plunger for a motor car tyre.

Several witnesses came forward to support Lethbridge's story. In Salisbury Road, Cathays, Cardiff, residents said that on the same evening, between 10.40 and 10.50 p.m., they had also seen an airship-like object in the air.

CIGAR-SHAPED

Additional testimony came from Cardiff dockers who, two hours after Lethbridge's encounter, saw a fast moving 'boat of cigar shape' flying from the direction of Newport, and going eastwards. The airship carried two lights, and its engines made a loud whirring noise. One witness said: 'We could not see those on board. The airship was too high up for that at night, but it was plain that it was a big airship.'

Two gentlemen made some even more extravagant claims, to the effect that they had seen a 200-230 foot (60-70 metre) long airship 'like a collection of big cigar boxes with the ends out' on Ham Common, London. The occupants of the craft, whom they met on the night of 13 May, were described as a clean-shaven Yankee and a German who smoked a calabash pipe. The German asked for some tobacco, which one of the witnesses supplied out of his own pouch. Although they were blinded by a searchlight that played on their faces, the witnesses were able to see that the 'Yankee' was positioned in a kind of wire cage: in front of him, he had a row of levers similar to draught beer pump handles. In front of the German was positioned a map with pins dotted all over it. The encounter apparently came to an abrupt end when the 'Yankee' pulled one of the levers down. Then he switched the light off, and the craft flew off, without either of the men saying good-bye.

With such a variety of bizarre reports, it is hardly surprising that the mystery of the phantom scareships that plagued Britain in 1909 has proved so difficult to solve.

" IN EVERY THOUSAND MEN, THERE ARE ALWAYS TWO EVERY NIGHT WHO SEE STRANGE MATTERS. "

THE LOST HOUR

One quiet evening, Linda Taylor was driving her mother home, when they were startled to see a UFO hovering above their car

Linda Taylor points out to UFO researcher Harry Harris, precisely where she saw the alien craft.

I t was 10 January 1982. My mother and I had left Southport, Lancashire, at 7 pm, and about half-an-hour later, I was driving along the East Lancashire Road. We were talking, when we suddenly became aware of a huge light over the road and behind some trees. It was a very bright, white light. It seemed to be making some strange movements – that was what drew our attention to it – and we wondered what on earth it could be. At first, I thought it could be one of those radio-controlled aeroplanes, which had got out of control. The light suddenly went zig-zagging, shooting up in the sky at strange angles, appearing and disappearing until I lost sight of it completely. My mother was in the back seat, and I asked her if she could see it behind us, but she said she could not.

Then the most bizarre thing happened. All of a sudden, I started to lose speed, but I wasn't trying to. So I changed down into third gear, still losing speed, and now the car started vibrating: the lights were going on and off, and the indicator lights started flashing. I was very concerned and thought we were going to break down. It was a very quiet stretch of road, and there were no lights there.

The next thing that happened was that an old-fashioned, 1930s-style black car appeared in front of me. It just appeared from nowhere! I presume the driver was a man because he was a very large figure, with broad shoulders. He was dressed in dark clothing, and wore a sort of bowler hat. The car's back-bumper was almost touching my front-bumper. It had no lights on, and it had no registration plates, but I could tell it was old because of the small oval window at the back. It was as though it was a magnet attaching itself to my car. My mother was saying: 'Look out, we're going to crash, we're going to hit it!'

Now I changed down into second gear to try to avoid crashing, but I wasn't in control at all. I opened the window, thinking to shout at the man in front, so I wound down my window, and then I saw the light again. I looked up and there it was – a UFO. It wasn't a projection from my mind, it wasn't a fantasy, it wasn't a ball of gas, a helicopter or an aeroplane: it was a UFO.

It was covered in lights – they were about five feet in diameter, and all different colours. I screamed and put my head back inside the car. Immediately I did that, the car in front just vanished. I put my foot down, still in second gear, and the car lurched forward. Up ahead, I could see the lights of a petrol station, just before the M63 motorway. I pulled in and got out of the car.

❝ IT WASN'T A PROJECTION FROM MY MIND ... IT WASN'T A BALL OF GAS, A HELICOPTER OR AN AEROPLANE: IT WAS A UFO. ❞

My mother and I looked back in the direction we had come from, and there it was, a huge light in the sky. We were standing by a covered garage. Anybody inside the garage wouldn't have been able to see out into the sky. There was a man about to put petrol into his car; and just before he saw it, the UFO came over the top of the covered garage. Now, I remember it as having circled the garage three times, but my mother thinks it only went round once. But, as this was happening, it felt as though all time stood still. It was a very peculiar feeling. There was no sound, just nothingness. It was travelling quite low over the garage, and stopped above a tree. It made a quick movement, tilted, and started to vibrate. But still there was no noise. We just watched it rise up.

It was only when we got home that I realised that it was nearly an hour later than it should have been. Somewhere we had lost a whole chunk of time. I dropped off my mother in Hume, and drove back to my husband in Chorlton.

By the time I got home, I was feeling nauseous and was shaking all over. I knocked on the front door, too upset to use my key. My husband came to the door, took one look at me, and said 'You've had an accident'. I said 'Phone my mother, I can't talk, she'll tell you what's happened'. Then I went into the bathroom, was violently sick, and discovered my legs were covered in strange black and red marks that disappeared the day after.

I asked my mother if we should report it but she said: 'Who'll believe us? The papers will just take the mickey out of us, and the police will think we're crazy'. It was only when I was watching the television, some nine months later, that I saw an interview with members of a local UFO group. I wrote to the programme-makers, who put me in touch with UFO researchers, Mike Sacks and Harry Harris. They had been involved in running hypnotic regression sessions with other UFO witnesses who had suffered amnesia after their sightings. It was a great relief to tell somebody about my experience, without the fear of being ridiculed.

Now, nearly ten years later, I still find it a very distressing experience. I've been hypnotically regressed, but it couldn't unlock my memories of the missing hour. It did reaffirm, however, that whatever happened to me was a very frightening experience as I get extremely distressed whilst under hypnosis. I'll never know what happened. Did they take me and my mother into their spacecraft, and experiment on us? I feel like the victim of something awful or sinister that took place during the hour that they stole from my life. How dare they!

One thing the hypnotic regression did reveal was that I arrived home without my coat. And that had completely been blanked out of my mind. So maybe someone up there has still got it.

I've since become very interested in the whole area of ufology, and joined Harry Harris as a researcher. I still look out at the sky every night and wonder where they come from and whether they're going to come back. I believe they're very real, physical beings, who have total control over the human mind.

I have written to the Ministry of Defence, to see if there were any unusual radar sightings that day, or whether they knew anything about the craft, but they have been very unforthcoming.

UFOs: THE CASE FOR A COVER-UP

The US government has long denied any interest in UFOs, yet it keeps thousands of UFO documents on the secret list. Here we report on a bizarre CIA plot, apparently to mislead the public

An unidentified flying object skims over the desert outside Phoenix, Arizona, on 12 September 1972. Checked by computerized enhancement techniques, the photograph has been declared genuine by Ground Saucer Watch. Despite such evidence, government agencies such as the CIA – whose official seal appears above – deny the existence of UFOs.

UFO researchers have long maintained that their governments know more about the UFO phenomenon than they officially admit. One reason for thinking this has been the unfailingly sceptical attitude taken by government officials when questioned about any particular sighting – even the best-documented reports are greeted with cries of 'weather balloons' or 'the planet Venus seen under unusual conditions'. Another cause for suspicion has been the peculiar interest that UFOs take in military establishments from time to time. Some, at least, of the infamous 'men in black' (MIBs) may have been genuine government agents, and the thought may linger in many ufologists' minds that the MIB's elusive nature is only the

smoke of folklore, behind which lurks the sinister fire of clandestine operations. In the United States, the idea of deliberate government attack on ufology was confirmed for many by the publication in 1969 of the Condon Report, widely regarded as, at best, complacent or, at worst, wilfully ignorant.

Documents obtained by Ground Saucer Watch (GSW) from the United States government under the Freedom of Information Act now confirm that there has indeed been a cover-up – right from the start of the modern UFO era in the late 1940s. But what is revealed by the documents is not that there is a world-wide plot to hide the true nature of UFOs – involving secret contact with extra-terrestrials or some gruesome conspiracy against humanity, or

be identified, were sufficient information on each sighting available. How can the man in the street argue with logic like that?

SCREEN OF DENIALS

The debunking campaign has been successful, too, because well-known military or government figures have weighed in against the UFO. Most people have an automatic respect for public figures, and so their statements are readily accepted. The few researchers who believed that they saw through the screen of official denials were therefore easily dismissed as mavericks or cranks. There was, according to the official line, nothing to research. The government knew about everything there was to be seen in the sky.

But perhaps the cover-up was itself so successful because no one could prove it was going on. There was also no hard evidence to back the claim that the government was not being completely honest with the public. Then again, if governments know so much, why have more ex-employees not come forward with their stories – revelations that are far more explosive, potentially, than any political scandal?

Despite all this, one's suspicions remain. Over the years, Ground Saucer Watch (GSW) has encountered numerous incidents that showed

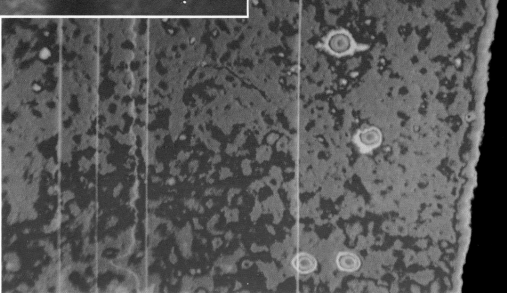

A still from the film shot by Delbert C. Newhouse on 2 July 1952, 7 miles (11 kilometres) north of Tremonton, Utah, USA, is reproduced above. Newhouse saw 'gunmetal coloured objects shaped like two saucers, one inverted on top of the other', near the eastern horizon. Mystified, he shot some 16-millimetre film of them. A few frames have been released to the public, but many more remain in CIA hands. Ground Saucer Watch (GSW) analysed the available frames with a range of techniques that included colour contrasting, right. This demonstrated that the objects were indeed solid. Sceptics have claimed the UFOs were birds or planes, but computerised images of these at comparable distances – centre right, a bird; far right, a plane – show quite different characteristics of shape, reflectivity and density. GSW concluded that the images in Newhouse's film represented craft about 50 feet (15 metres) in diameter and 5–7 miles (8–11 kilometres) distant.

some other outlandish suggestion. What is indicated, rather, is that the US government wishes to maintain a certain public attitude towards UFOs for its own reasons.

This atmosphere of doubt and derision has been created in a number of ways. Anyone can offer more or less plausible explanations for a UFO sighting: bright planets, unusual atmospheric conditions, meteorites, aircraft and so on. This approach cannot help but be successful, since as many as 95 per cent of alleged UFOs are indeed misinterpretations of known objects. Some sceptical investigators even maintain that if these statistics are valid, then all UFO reports must represent objects that could

every sign of direct or indirect government interference. Photographs went missing; ground markings were ploughed under; occasional witnesses talked about visits from military or intelligence officers who wanted to suppress the stories of their UFO encounters. Too many cases came to an abrupt halt because some of the evidence was missing, making it impossible to reach a firm conclusion.

Largely at the insistence of Todd Zechel of GSW, it was decided to attack the issue head on and approach the government directly. In the first instance, GSW questioned the US Air Force – with predictable results. Typical replies were that 'the phenomenon does not represent any advanced technology beyond our present capability and... poses no direct threat to the United States,' and that 'there is no evidence indicating that sightings categorized as "unidentified" are extraterrestrial vehicles.' This was no more than had been expected. The next step was to confront the CIA – most likely to be involved in suppressing UFO material. The CIA's reply to GSW dated 26 March 1976 is intriguing in the light of later events:

'In order that you may be aware of the true facts concerning the involvement of the CIA in the investigation of UFO phenomena, let me give you the following brief history. Late in 1952, the National Security Council levied upon the CIA the requirement to determine if the existence of UFOs would create a danger to the security of the United States. The Office of Scientific Intelligence established the Intelligence Advisory Committee to study the matter. That committee made the recommendations in the Robertson Panel Report. At no time prior to the formation of the Robertson Panel, and subsequent to this issuance of the panel's report [in January 1953], has the CIA engaged in the study of UFO phenomena. The Robinson Panel Report is the summation of the Agency's interest and involvement in this matter.'

The Panel's conclusions – after an intensive briefing by top airmen, astronomers and several CIA

Research director Todd Zechel, above left, and director William H. Spaulding, right, of Ground Saucer Watch, are seen discussing the UFO problem.

men – was that there was no cause for alarm, but the panel concluded that 'the continued emphasis on the reporting of these phenomena does, in these perilous times, result in a threat to the orderly functioning of the protective organs of the body politic.' Their recommendations were framed accordingly – debunk UFOs and educate people to recognise aerial phenomena.

In fact, the CIA did not let the matter drop there in 1953. Searches through the National Archives showed that many reports were missing from the files. When GSW made specific requests under the Freedom of Information Act, a few papers were released, but they were so highly 'sanitized' that only a mind-reader could have made sense of them. GSW then decided to attack in the courts. After 14 months of gruelling legal action, the government released, on 15 December 1978, close to 1,000 pages of documents. It was a major victory.

PSYCHOLOGICAL WARFARE

What do the papers show? Firstly, they indicate that CIA involvement in UFOs actually pre-dates the National Security Council directive to set up what became the Robertson Panel. Indeed, it seems it was the CIA that urged an investigation on the Council! Secondly, the implications for psychological warfare clearly attracted considerable attention. As one memo puts it: 'A fair proportion of our population is mentally conditioned to the acceptance of the incredible. In this fact lies the potential for the touching-off of mass hysteria and panic.' The third concern is with the vulnerability of US air defences: 'At any moment of attack... we cannot... distinguish hardware from phantom... ' The use of the word 'phantom' is interesting, for another memo, from the Deputy Director for Intelligence, CIA, dated November 1952, says bluntly: 'Sightings of unexplained objects at great altitudes and travelling at high speeds in the vicinity of major US defense installations are of such a nature that they are not attributable to natural phenomena or known types of aerial vehicles.'

In the light of that, it is not surprising that when Edward Tauss, then Acting Chief of the Weapons and Equipment Division of the Office of Scientific Intelligence, recommended that the CIA 'continue' (not 'begin') coverage of the subject in August 1952, he should add: 'It is strongly urged, however, that no indication of CIA interest or concern

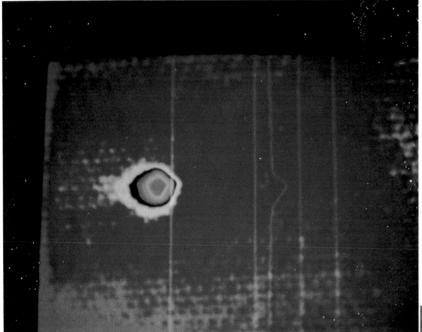

❚❚ IT IS CLEAR THAT THE CIA

AT LEAST BELIEVED IN THE

REALITY OF UFO PHENOMENA.

IT WAS ALSO ALARMED BY IT.

AND IT WAS DETERMINED TO

KEEP WHAT IT DID KNOW

TO ITSELF. **❚❚**

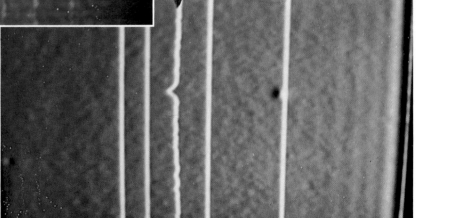

The view of the Earth's surface, **above,** shows the blue glow of the atmosphere at the horizon, cloud formations and, apparently, a small round UFO, to the right of the picture.

Taken by astronaut M. Scott Carpenter from **Aurora 7,** 1,000 miles (1,600 kilometres) above the Earth, this picture has been acclaimed as conclusive evidence for rumours about the frequent 'buzzing' of NASA space capsules by UFOs. But in fact, the object following this capsule so attentively is an IFO (Identified Flying Object) – the meteorological balloon towed behind the capsule.

The two frames, **left** and **below,** are from a ciné film of unidentified lights that were seen over Stonehenge by the families of John Flattley and a friend on 18 October 1977. They described silent, erratically moving lights. Sometimes as many as seven or eight were clearly visible. At one point, the lights seemed to hang motionless in the sky for long periods. The nearby Army base has been blamed for the lights, but witnesses state that they adamantly reject the explanation of military flares. Could the Army perhaps be responsible for something more sinister?

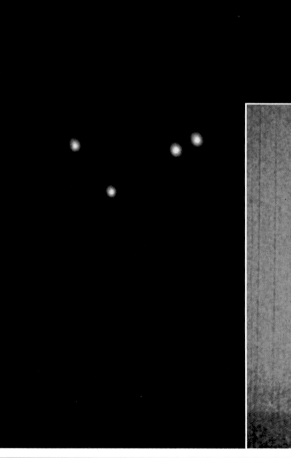

The UFO, **above** and **right,** was captured on ciné film on the morning of 11 January 1973 by Peter Day, on the road close to Cuddington (between Thame and Aylesbury, England). He had been watching the UFO for about a minute before he was able to park his car and then use his 8-millimetre ciné camera to record it. The object emerged from behind the trees and travelled horizontally from left to right at a low altitude. Peter Day said the UFO seemed to be flickering or pulsating; this is reflected in the difference in brightness of the object between the two consecutive frames of his film, shown here. He 'caught' the object for 15 seconds only as it zoomed across the tops of the trees. Although he was alone during the sighting, a number of children and teachers at a school some miles away confirmed the sudden appearance and abrupt disappearance of a UFO at approximately the same time as his sighting. The **Thame Gazette** of 16 January 1973 quoted one of the children who described the object as 'a huge blob of orange fire'. The UFO was said to have approached within a few hundred yards of the school, illuminating the ground with a bright orange glow as it passed by. One of the teachers told Peter Day that the object had hung motionless above and ahead of her for a few seconds. She noted that it looked like a ball at the top, but was flat at the bottom, and the whole object was spinning.

Ciné films of UFOs – such as those shown here – are important for a number of reasons: imagination on the part of the witnesses can be ruled out entirely; a moving object is extremely difficult to fake; and relative distances – of the object and trees, houses, the Sun or stars, for example – can be more easily estimated than from a still photograph. The usual 'explanations' – flocks of birds, the planet Venus and weather balloons – can be eliminated; and the moving pictures can be 'frozen', frame by frame, for analysis.

WHEN LIGHT BEAMS BEND

THE ABILITY OF UFOS TO DEFLECT LIGHT BEAMS, THEREBY DEFYING ALL KNOWN PHYSICAL LAWS, ARE REPORTED IN THE TWO CASES PRESENTED HERE, FROM AUSTRALIA AND FRANCE

Sullivan's headlight beams bent sharply and mysteriously to the right, as depicted in the artist's impression, above.

Newcomers to ufological research, accustomed to conventional physics, often throw up their hands in incredulity when they are confronted with reports of the extraordinary phenomena that sometimes occur during UFO sightings. Among the most remarkable of these are accounts of beams of light that stop short or make abrupt bends, without any evident absorbing, refracting or reflecting agencies to bring this about. In the two cases discussed here, beams from torches and car headlamps seem to have been manipulated in an equally 'impossible' way.

The London *Daily Express* of 12 April 1966 carried a story in which it reported that a motorist, 38-year-old Ronald Sullivan, had been cruising along near Bendigo in southern Australia under a moonlit sky when he noticed that, inexplicably, his headlight beams suddenly bent to the right. In a statement made to the police at Maryborough, near Melbourne, he said that he avoided a crash only with difficulty and, as he drew to a halt, saw a display of 'gaseous lights' of all colours of the rainbow in a field alongside the road. The display, he said, was followed by the appearance of an object that rose vertically to a point about 10 feet (3 metres) in the air and then just disappeared.

When Sullivan returned to the scene a few days later, he found that another motorist, Gary Turner, had been killed in a crash at the same spot the previous evening. Meanwhile, the police had made their investigations and found, in a freshly ploughed field 50 feet (20 metres) from the fence, a circular depression about 5 feet (1.5 metres) across, and varying from 2 to 5 inches (5–13 centimetres) in depth. The police regarded Sullivan – a highly respected businessman – as a reliable witness, and noted that he professed not to believe in UFOs.

The *Daily Express* story ended there. The corresponding Associated Press message was more detailed, however: apparently, Sullivan's encounter took place on 4 April 1966; he returned to the site on 8 April, and it was then that he learned of the fatal accident that had taken place on 7 April. A report in the *Melbourne Herald* added that he had driven to nearby Wycheproof where he had had his headlights checked – they were found to be in perfect working order – before going on to the police.

It was also revealed that the bent beam incident and the fatal accident occurred on a long straight stretch of road between Bendigo and St Arnaud, at a point 9 miles (15 kilometres) east of Bealiba, a small town nearly 130 miles (210 kilometres) northwest of Melbourne.

The information that was available left it a matter of speculation as to whether the bending of the headlight beams was accidentally caused by Sullivan's car running into the UFO's 'force field' or whether, if the incidents of 4 and 7 April were connected in some way, the bending was the result of a deliberate action by a hostile agency – whether it be human or alien.

FREAK REFLECTIONS

In a commentary in *Flying Saucer Review*, scientist Stephen L. Smith deplored the absence of important detail such as the make of Sullivan's car, the kind of dipping mechanism employed in its headlights, and the exact position on the beams at which they were bent. He pointed out that there were three possible explanations: that the beams were bent at source, that the bending occurred somewhere along the beams, or that the beams appeared bent through illusion or hallucination. Smith wrote that his colleagues of the Cambridge University Investigation Group had suggested how an illusion might be brought about by the sudden extinguishing of the left-hand component of the headlight beam which 'through its divergent character would seem to have been bent to the right . . . [due] to a freak of reflection caused by the absence of dust particles by which headlight beams are normally seen'.

There are other possibilities, too. If hallucination were the cause of the phenomenon, then perhaps it was spontaneously generated in the witness's brain. Or was it caused by some outside agency – perhaps a force field emanating from the object that he had observed?

The second case we highlight occurred some 6 miles (10 kilometres) north of Cluny in eastern France, on 12 August 1972. The day before, people from all walks of life – most of them young folk – had gathered at the Protestant monastery at Taizé for celebrations organized by its founder, Friar Roger Schutz.

The events at Taizé in the early hours of 12 August 1972 were reported to the gendarmerie at Cluny, and afterwards to the French UFO organisation *Lumières dans la Nuit,* for whom an investigation was conducted by a schoolmaster named Tyrode.

According to the report, a group of about 35 young people had collected for discussions at a rustic open air theatre situated among the visitors' tents near the crest of a ridge on which the community's buildings also stood. This site faced westwards over a gently sloping valley, and a ridge known as La Cras, and successively higher ridges beyond that. The sky was overcast, and a light drizzle soon began to fall.

From the place where the earnest young debaters were grouped, a large ploughed field sloped down into the valley. F. Tantot, from Mâcon, a young man from Dijon and an Italian student were alerted at about 2 a.m. by Renata, from Sardinia, to a 'star' that she could see descending. Before the others could swing round, however, she was already telling them that it had 'landed'. In a few moments, all the people in the theatre could see an object, seemingly stationary, on the slopes of La Cras, facing them and at the same level as themselves. All present had also heard the whistling noise as the UFO approached, and they could now see that it was bounded to the left by a field of cereal – its light colour showed up the UFO as dark by contrast – and to the right by a large tree standing on the ridge. The size of the UFO was estimated as 'larger than a coach'.

All the witnesses now saw the UFO 'light up'. Seven yellow lights appeared in a row, then two orange ones outside and to the left of the object.

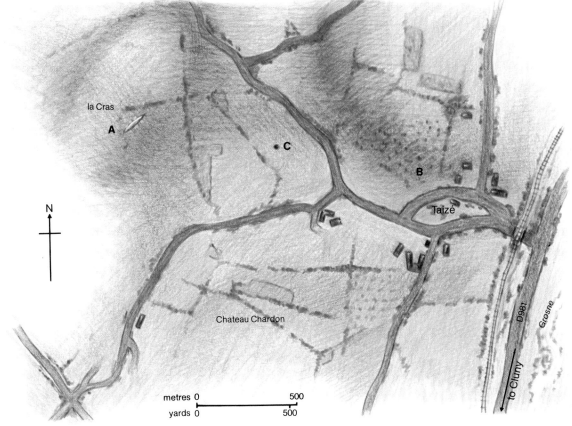

By now, the intrepid four had reached the middle of the field, and they became aware of a dark, haystack-shaped mass some 6 or 7 yards (5 or 6 metres) high, around which a point of red light moved in a haphazard trajectory. Between themselves and this mass, the witnesses thought they could see a hedge about 10 feet (3 metres) ahead – but at a point where, they knew, no hedge existed. When a torch beam was shone towards the mass, the beam suddenly turned vertically upwards about 1½ feet (50 centimetres) from the hedge and, dispersing, was soon lost in the air.

Subsequent attempts to illuminate the object, using all the torches the witnesses had with them, met with the same fate and, alarmed, the four were tempted to back off. However, when the lights on the UFO suddenly went out, only to flash back on again, and the three discs vanished into the big object, Tantot flashed his torch in that direction. As if in response, the largest beam from the UFO rose so that it shone directly at the witnesses. Dazzled, and feeling a surge of heat, they raised their hands to protect their eyes. Meanwhile, the UFO began to move away, suddenly accelerating towards Cluny. It was 4.40 a.m when the craft was finally lost from sight at Taizé.

The Taizé UFO, above, is shown emitting white pylon-like beams. In the field, below, a red light leaves a bright, looping trajectory around the haystack-shaped mass. The witnesses' torch beams, meanwhile, bend inexplicably up into the air.

After that, five of the yellow lights began to emit beams that extended slowly towards the ground. What appeared to be cupolas were also observed above the two light beams at the very left of the row. When discussing the phenomenon, some witnesses said they had the impression that the beams were pylons on which the object was supported. Indeed, it was as if the beams were made of solid matter. At this point, some of the witnesses, particularly Tantot and the man from Dijon, felt tingling in their fingers and knees.

GYRATING LIGHTS

While the 'solid' beams of light were extending to the ground, a train of red sparks was seen at the right-hand end of the object. These were soon extinguished; and where they had been, there were now seen three small discs, each with two red points of light. These began to gyrate around the main UFO, and the manoeuvres went on until the end of the sighting.

At about 3 a.m., the four original witnesses decided to have a closer look at the big object and, armed with torches, set off across the field, watched as they went by the remaining 30 witnesses in the theatre, who were later able to report that the main beams were rotating around individual vertical axes. The beam second from the left suddenly grew brighter, and showers of red particles filled the air around the four and covered the ground. A row of what looked like portholes then appeared in white light, only to disappear after approximately 20 minutes, when the large beam to the left started to flash several times.

ROADS OF FEAR

CLOSE ENCOUNTERS WITH ALIEN ENTITIES ON LONELY ROADS ARE COMPARATIVELY FREQUENT OCCURRENCES AND KNOWN TO HAPPEN AS FAR APART AS FRANCE AND TASMANIA. STRANGELY, SOME SUCH EXPERIENCES EVEN OCCUR REPEATEDLY

One of the more curious aspects of the UFO phenomenon is the way in which certain individuals are sometimes singled out for more than one visitation. Our first story concerns one such 'repeater', who experienced UFO sightings and related phenomena for nearly 20 years, culminating in a terrifying encounter on a lonely road in southern France.

The second story is a close encounter of the second kind – with a difference. In addition to the interference with electrical equipment that has come to be regarded as normal in UFO sightings, there were more unusual side-effects: after the sighting, for instance, the witness noticed that the front of her car, which had been dirty, was as clean as if it had just been washed, and her hair, which had recently been treated with a permanent wave, went completely straight!

It was 10.45 p.m. on 29 August 1975 and R.Cyrus – a former policeman turned businessman, aged 48 – was driving along route D10 from Longages to a point south of Noé where the road joins Route Nationale 125. It is a country district, deep in the Haute-Garonne region of south-western France. The sky was clear, the weather was mild, and a light south-east wind was blowing. Under a bright moon, he had travelled about three-quarters of the way along the road when he observed, in a field to the right, an aluminium-coloured machine. When, a second or two later, he was almost level with this object, the underpart became illuminated with a phosphorescent glow, and it floated in the air, at bonnet height, towards the front of the car.

Cyrus rammed on the brakes just as the object tilted back to present its underside to the driver. At that moment, the luminosity increased enormously and, blinded by the fierce light, Cyrus threw up his arms to protect his head and eyes. His car swerved

A blinding white light shone towards the car, as shown left in the artist's impression, and finally forced the witness into a ditch.

As depicted in the illustration, above, a beam of light, reddish in tinge, illuminated Cyrus car, but not the surrounding area.

home!' It was a statement that subsequently puzzled him. His wife later said that, when he arrived home, he was utterly distraught.

When questioned, Cyrus said he could not recall having been 'paralysed' by the UFO's presence, but he did remember that his throat was all 'jammed up', and he was unable to utter a sound until the motorist opened the car door. There were other physiological effects, too. After the encounter, the witness experienced bouts of sleepiness, even when driving; whenever he stopped doing anything, he found himself falling asleep. His eyesight, too, was briefly affected: when awakening on the two mornings following his experience, he had black spots before the eyes, but these gradually faded.

Surprisingly, there were no signs of burns or scratches, nor changes of colour on the car after the event. And there was another unusual feature about the sighting: the engine did not stall during the event, and the lights continued to work normally throughout.

Attempts were made by investigators to locate landing marks, but nothing was found. Aerial photographs also failed to reveal anything.

It was unfortunate that the motorist who approached Cyrus after the sighting presumably declined to make a statement, and refused to allow his name to be mentioned. There were, however, two other independent but vague reports of lights in the sky, and of one in a field some distance from the road.

During the course of their investigation for the French UFO organisation *Lumières dans la Nuit* (Lights in the Night), the researchers, a certain M.Cattiau and his colleagues, greatly assisted by the good-natured collaboration of Cyrus, unearthed the remarkable fact that he appeared to be one of the group of witnesses known as 'repeaters': it transpired that he had been through at least three earlier UFO experiences.

In 1957, he had been at a vineyard at Quillan in Aude, south-west France, during the grape harvest, when he saw, at about 8.30 one evening, two orange-coloured, cigar-shaped objects some 200 yards (180 metres) away. They were hovering over rows of vines while a cart passed below, its driver apparently oblivious to what was happening. Cyrus had called other vineyard workers from their dinner. When they saw the intruders, they ran towards them, whereupon the objects departed silently.

Again, one midnight in the autumn of 1974, Cyrus had been driving with his wife from Noé to the town of Muret when they saw a strange object to their left. It seemed to be composed of flashes of light, but these were suddenly succeeded by a huge orange sphere that illuminated the countryside, and kept pace with their car for about 5 miles (8 kilometres). When they arrived at the village of Ox, they were able to compare its size with that of the church: the sphere appeared enormous. Then, as they passed, a nearby transformer appeared to explode. It was confirmed next day that the circuit-breaker had tripped during the night for some unknown reason.

Twice in 1975, a few weeks before the encounter of 29 August, Cyrus also stated that he heard guttural voices speaking in an unidentifiable

off the road and ended up in a shallow ditch. Even as that happened, the UFO shot straight up and hovered, as a bright point of light in the sky, directly above the car. All this took place in the space of five seconds or so, and there was no sound whatsoever from the UFO.

For a moment, Cyrus sat motionless, getting out of his car only when a passing motorist stopped nearby and came over to open the door for him. 'I thought your car was exploding,' the motorist said.

The former gendarme, shocked and unsteady, touched himself 'to see if he was still alive'. Then he muttered: 'Good heavens – is this it?'

Meanwhile, the light of the UFO, high above, was fluctuating in intensity, and had taken on a reddish tinge. Cyrus stood where he was, watching the phenomenon for some 15 minutes. A compact beam shone down from the object, illuminating the car but not the surrounding area.

By now, a number of people had arrived on the scene, and the consensus of opinion was that Cyrus should report the matter immediately to the gendarmerie. But he declared: 'You all know me; I'll go to the gendarmerie tomorrow. Now I'm off language on his car radio each time he had the radio switched off. While this is not strictly within the UFO realm, some investigations have been forced to wonder whether or not Cyrus is a deep-trance subject, or perhaps possesses a degree of clairvoyance – in which case, something could well have been 'beamed in' on him, setting him up for the big encounter of 29 August.

TASMANIAN ENCOUNTER

A year previously, a Tasmanian woman, who wishes to remain anonymous, experienced a not dissimilar phenomenon. Late on the afternoon of 22 September 1974, she arrived at the junction of the Diddleum and Tayene Plains roads, around 30 miles (50 kilometres) north-east of Launceston. It was raining, and the mountains were shrouded in mist as she parked her car around 200 yards (180 metres) from the junction and waited for the arrival of the relative she was due to pick up. Because there was a steep bank to the left of the road, she parked her car on the other side to ensure that any of the heavy log trucks that frequently used the narrow road would see the vehicle clearly.

Over the car radio, she heard that the time was 5.20 p.m. Then, suddenly, the radio developed a high-pitched whine and the whole landscape lit up, bright light flooding the inside of the car. She leaned over to switch off the radio and, looking up through the windscreen, saw a glowing orange and

The UFO, below, was seen by a woman on a Tasmanian road in 1974. It was silver-grey, and featured several wide bands beneath a dome that emitted an intense orange-yellow light.

silver object moving between two trees and coming downhill towards her. It was the size of a large car, moving slowly 50-60 feet (15-18 metres) above the ground, and dropping steadily towards the road.

Not surprisingly, the woman panicked. She started the car and hurriedly began to reverse up the road, away from the UFO. But the object went on approaching until it was at the level of the fence at the side of the road. It then hovered over the middle of the road about 30-35 yards (25-30 metres) from the woman's car. It appeared to be domed on top, although it was difficult to make out its exact shape because of the intense orange-yellow light that it emitted. Beneath the dome, the UFO was silver-grey in colour. There was also a wide band on which the witness said there could have been portholes, and six to eight horizontal bands below it, decreasing in diameter. At the bottom of the object was a small revolving disc, and below this what appeared to be a box or tube, which protruded from the base a short way.

After reversing about 100 yards (90 metres), the woman accidentally backed the car over the edge of the road, and the wheel stuck fast. The UFO now stopped in front of the witness. It then dipped to the right and moved away to the south-west over a valley beside the road. It next rose vertically upwards, fairly quickly, until lost from vision. The entire sighting had lasted 3 to 4 minutes.

The witness jumped out of her car and ran all the way to her house, about a mile (1.6 kilometres) away. All the while, she had the feeling that she was being watched, and kept looking up to see if the UFO was following her: she did not, however, see anything. When she arrived home, her husband and son went to inspect the car. They could see nothing unusual.

The next day, however, when the car was towed home, it was noticed that the front of the car was exceptionally clean, although the rest of it was as dirty as it had been before the encounter. Previously, there had been cat footprints all over the bonnet, but it seemed to have been given a good polish. It appeared impossible that the rain of the previous day could have cleaned the front of the car while leaving the back dirty.

STATE OF SHOCK

For some days after her terrifying experience, the witness was ill with nervous tension and seemed in a state of shock. Her hair, which had been newly treated with a permanent wave, turned straight after her encounter. Furthermore, the car radio, which had been in perfect working order before the sighting, afterwards suffered from distortion. This, of course, is a common phenomenon in close encounters with UFOs.

The witness initially reported the sighting to the Royal Australian Air Force (RAAF), who could not supply her with any explanation, but they ruled out such things as weather balloons, aircraft, and meteorological phenomena. The case was also investigated by the northern representative of the Tasmanian UFO Investigation Centre, and subsequently reported to *Flying Saucer Review*. As yet, however, we do not know whether this particular individual's experience will be repeated.

UFO
PHOTO FILE

The 'long object with a hump on its back', **above,** was photographed over Bear Mountain in New York State by an anonymous witness on 18 December 1966. The sighting was reported to the US Air Force's Project Blue Book who took possession of two photographs and a negative, and also held exhaustive interviews with the witness. Although the US Air Force's own technicians could find no evidence of fraud, the file was nevertheless labelled 'Hoax'. Dr. J. Allen Hynek wrote to Major Hector Quintanilla (then Chief of Project Blue Book) saying: '... the lack of satisfactory explanation of the unidentified object does not constitute sufficient reason to declare [it] a hoax... My recommendation is... that the evaluation be changed from hoax to unidentified'. Despite this recommendation, the 'Hoax' label has remained.

The two frames, **below** and **below left,** are from a film said to be of 'an approaching UFO', and were taken by Daniel W. Fry during May 1964 near his home in Merlin, Oregon, using a 16-millimetre Bell and Howell movie camera. The UFO, described by Fry as 'spinning like a top during flight', was by no means the first alien craft Fry claimed to have encountered. It was, according to him, some 14 years previously, in 1950, that he had witnessed his first 'flying saucer' landing, and during the next four years he claims he was a contactee of beings described by him as 'the Space People'. They allegedly told him that they are the descendants of a lost super-race originally from Earth who survived a nuclear holocaust over 30,000 years ago and fled to live on Mars. Later they abandoned Mars and now live exclusively in their spacecraft.

Another 'Martian spacecraft', photographed by Daniel W. Fry, with the same movie camera, is shown **above right** and **right.** The time is May 1965 and the place, Joshua Tree, California. This craft was also described as 'spinning like a top' in the sky. Fry, a former employee of the Aerojet General Corporation (where he was 'in charge of installation of instruments for missile control and guidance'), is considered to be the most technically orientated of modern contactees. Sceptics have pointed out, however, that this technical background might also provide him with opportunities to produce fake photographs of a high standard, but there is no conclusive evidence that these two images are fakes.

FLYING SAUCERS ON FILM

Late in the evening of 30 December 1978, an Argosy freight plane set off from Wellington, New Zealand. Its skipper was Captain Bill Startup, who had 23 years' flying experience behind him, and the co-pilot was Bob Guard. On board were an Australian TV crew from Channel 0-10 Network; reporter, Quentin Fogarty; and camera-man, David Crockett and his wife, sound recordist Ngaire Crockett. Their purpose was to film UFOs, for there had been reports of 'unknowns' during the preceding weeks in the region of Cook Strait, which separates New Zealand's North and South Islands. They were spectacularly successful in the quest, so successful in fact that, after the story had appeared in hundreds of newspapers and clips from the films had been shown repeatedly on television around the world – the BBC, for instance, gave it pride of place on the main evening news – critics and droves of debunkers lined up to try to explain what the television crew had seen, in terms ranging from the sublimely astronomical to the ridiculously absurd.

The Argosy had crossed Cook Strait and was fly-ing over the Pacific Ocean off the north-east coast of South Island when the excitement began. The television crew was down by the loading bay, film-ing 'intros' with Quentin Fogarty, when Captain Startup called over the intercom for them to hurry to the flight deck: the pilots had seen some strange objects in the sky. According to Crockett, they had already checked with Wellington air traffic control for radar confirmation of their visual sighting.

Fogarty stated that, when he reached the flight deck, he saw a row of five bright lights. Large and brilliant, although a long way off, they were seen to

ONE OF THE MOST IMPRESSIVE UFO SIGHTINGS OF ALL TIME TOOK PLACE WHEN A NEW ZEALAND TELEVISION CREW MADE TWO FLIGHTS IN ORDER TO SEARCH FOR UFOS, AND ACTUALLY SUCCEEDED IN MAKING A FILM OF THEM

The spinning, luminous sphere above, was filmed by a New Zealand television crew on the night of 30 December 1978. The crew made two flights, looking for UFOs, on the same night and saw them both times.

pulsate, growing from pinpoint size to that of a large balloon full of glowing light. The sequence was then repeated, the objects appearing above the street lights of the town of Kaikoura, but between the aircraft and the ground.

UNKNOWN TARGET

Crockett, who was wearing headphones, received a call from Wellington control, warning the pilots that an unknown target was following the Argosy. Captain Startup put his plane into a turn to look for the unidentified object but the passengers and crew saw nothing. Control, however, was insistent: 'Sierra Alpha Eagle... you have a target in formation with you... target has increased in size.' This time, lights were seen outside the plane; but because of interference from the navigation lights of the plane, Crockett was unable to film. So First Officer Bob Guard switched off the navigation lights, and every-one saw a big, bright light. The plane was now back on automatic pilot, so Guard gave up his seat for Crockett, who obtained a clear shot of the object with his hand-held camera. Crockett has since

PERSPECTIVES

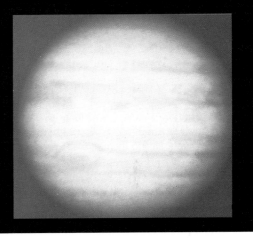

television crew had seen 'refections from moonlight via cabbage leaves'.

A more reasonable explanation was that the films showed a planet – but which one was it? One newspaper claimed it was Venus, *left;* another said it was Jupiter, *below.* But even the quickest glance at the planets themselves show these explanations to be unlikely. The *Daily Telegraph,* surprisingly, printed a remarkably strong condemnation of the Venus theory: 'The scientist who suggested that all they (the television crew) were seeing was Venus on a particularly bright night can... be safely consigned to Bedlam' was the British paper's conviction.

ROGUE PLANETS?

For a time it was thought that the New Zealand films might provide solid scientific evidence for the existence of UFOs, since they seemed to offer instrumental evidence both on film and on radar. Whatever they were, the objects were not hallucinations. Scientists were quick to react by putting forward a whole range of alternative explanations of what the objects in the films might be. Some of their theories were wildly implausible: one even claimed that the

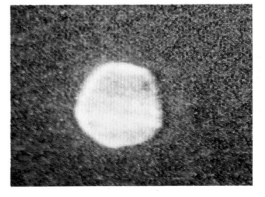

Two stills from the New Zealand television crew's film, right, show the presence of strange objects, as confirmed by Wellington air traffic control, who saw their traces on their radarscopes.

Captain Bill Startup, below, was pilot of the aircraft from which the UFO film was taken.

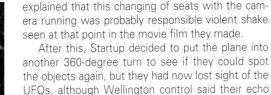

explained that this changing of seats with the camera running was probably responsible violent shake seen at that point in the movie film they made.

After this, Startup decided to put the plane into another 360-degree turn to see if they could spot the objects again, but they had now lost sight of the UFOs, although Wellington control said their echo was still on the radarscope.

Although there was no room for a camera tripod to be mounted on the flight deck, the unidentified object stayed steady enough for Crockett to be able to keep it dead centre in his camera viewfinder for more than 30 seconds.

As the plane approached Christchurch, the fuel gauge went into a spin, but the captain said that this occasionally happened and was not necessarily due to interference by the UFO. At this point, they were out of touch with Wellington control. Christchurch control, however, had the object on its radarscope but later, when Captain Startup and

American investigating scientist Dr Bruce Maccabee asked to see the radar tapes, the Christchurch supervisor replied that they had been 'wiped' clean as part of routine procedure.

The Argosy landed at Christchurch and journalist Dennis Grant joined the team in place of Dave Crockett's wife, Ngaire. They left on the return flight at about 2.15 a.m. on 31 December 1978.

PULSATING LIGHTS

Early in this flight, the observers saw two more strange objects. Through the camera lens, Crockett saw what he described as a sphere with lateral lines around it. This object focused itself as Crockett watched through his camera, without adjusting the lens. He said the sphere was spinning. Significantly, one of the objects swayed on the Argosy's weather radar continuously for some four minutes. Later, they all saw two pulsating lights, one of which suddenly fell in a blurred streak

A particularly intriguing type of UFO report concerns objects emerging from or disappearing into water – most often, the sea. One such well-documented instance is recorded in an extraordinary series of photographs taken in the Canary Islands in 1979. Some writers have even gone as far as to suggest that there are enormous UFO 'bases' hidden under the world's oceans. In the absence of any concrete evidence, however, we can only regard this as speculation.

All the cases that follow occurred within 200 miles (320 kilometres) of each other along the Brazilian coast, south of Rio de Janeiro, though they were all well-separated in time. All involved several witnesses and what appear to be 'nuts and bolts' craft. Only the Santos case seems amenable to a conventional explanation: but if witnesses were indeed confronted by a stray rocket, aircraft pod, or satellite debris, it seems strange that the authorities were unable to locate wreckage at the site of the crash.

On Sunday, 27 June 1970, Aristeu Machado and his five daughters were playing a game on the verandah of their home at 318 Avenida Niemeyer, Rio de Janeiro, from which they could look out over

It was from the verandah at their house in Avenida Niemeyer, above, which runs north-east along the coast near Rio de Janeiro, that the Machado family, their maid and a neighbour saw the strange craft and its occupants.

Aristeu Machado and his wife are seen, right, at the spot from which they watched the UFO, and subsequent events at sea.

the road below to the South Atlantic Ocean beyond. With them was their friend and neighbour João Aguiar, an official of the Brazilian Federal Police.

Maria Nazaré, their maid, who was preparing lunch in the kitchen, called out to check the time: it was 11.38 a.m. About two minutes after that, João Aguiar happened to look out over the sea, and quickly drew the attention of the others to 'a motor boat striking the water'. As this object descended, it threw up spray on all sides.

The game and lunch were quickly forgotten for, as the family and their guest watched the 'motor boat', they could see two 'bathers' aboard the craft:

they seemed to be signalling with their arms. In a statement to Dr Walter Buhler, who investigated the case, Aguiar said there were definitely two figures on board and that they were wearing 'shining clothing, and something on their heads'. The craft was a greyish metallic colour; it seemed to be between 15 and 20 feet (5 – 6 metres) in length and had a transparent cupola. One strange feature was noted: at no time did the object make the 'bobbing' movement associated with a boat on a swell.

João Aguiar ran down to the nearby Mar Hotel, and telephoned the harbour police. They promised to send help to the occupants of the 'motor boat', who were presumably involved in a mishap offshore. Aguiar then returned to the house and rejoined the Machados on their verandah. He had been away from the house for about 30 minutes.

FLASHING SEQUENCE

Shortly after Aguiar returned, the object – which was now seen to be disc-shaped – took off. It skimmed the water for some 300 yards (280 metres), throwing off a wave from the bows as it went. It now lifted from the sea and made off quickly towards the south-east. It was then that the witnesses realised it was not a motor boat but, rather, an object that looked like a flying saucer. A hexagonal-shaped appendage retracted into the underside of the main body, and a number of lights on the appendage flashed, in sequence – green, yellow, and then red.

Once airborne, the object appeared to be transparent rather than aluminium-coloured, and Maria Nazaré said she clearly saw two entities sitting inside. There was little traffic noise from the road at that time, but the witnesses could hear no sound from the object.

On the sea where the UFO had originally rested, the witnesses saw a white hoop-shaped object 'about the size of a trunk or chest', according to Maria Nazaré. Suddenly the hoop sank, then it reappeared and a yellow oval-shaped section separated from it. This, it was estimated, was some 16 inches (40 centimetres) across with about 8 inches (20 centimetres) projecting above the surface of the water. It remained stationary for about three minutes, then began to move towards the shore, with its longer axis directed at the witnesses. A green flange at the rear of the object separated from the main body and followed it at a distance of about a yard (1 metre). After 15 minutes, the yellow oval was about 130 yards (120 metres) from the shore, when it made a right-angled turn to its left and headed for the beach at Gávea – a movement directly opposed to the maritime current in the area at the time.

The white hoop disappeared several times; but when it came back into view, it was still pursuing its direct course for Gávea Beach, as though it were going to link up once again with the yellow object.

Meanwhile, the police launch from Fort Copacabana had arrived at the spot where the UFO had remained stationary, having come into view about 20 minutes after João Aguiar had gone to make his telephone call. So the crew must surely have seen the UFO take off. At roughly the position where the hoop had been left, the launch was seen to stop and the police hauled on board a strange red

The two-part craft, seen by Captain Rocha and his wife, is illustrated below.

cylindrical object, before making off at speed towards their base.

No statement was made by the police regarding what they saw or found. And, although an account of the incident appeared in the newspaper *Diário de Notícias* on 28 June 1970, no other witnesses came forward to confirm the sighting.

On 10 January 1958, Captain Chrysólogo Rocha

Eight-year-old Rute de Souza and a group of fishermen all saw the silvery object below, as it collided with the top of a palm tree.

was sitting with his wife in the porch of a house overlooking the sea near Curitiba, when he was surprised to see an unfamiliar 'island'. He had his binoculars focused on the piece of land and was amazed to see that it was growing in size. He cried out to people inside the house, and very soon eight of them joined the couple on the porch to witness the strange phenomenon.

The 'island' seemed to consist of two parts, one in the sea and the other suspended above it. Then, without warning, both parts sank out of sight. Soon afterwards, a steamer came into sight and passed very near the point where the objects were last seen. Fifteen minutes later, when the ship had gone, the 10 observers saw the objects appear to rise once again from the sea. Now they could see that the upper section was attached to the lower one by means of a number of shafts or tubes, which were quite bright. Up and down the shafts, small objects 'like beads in a necklace' passed in disorderly fashion. This second display lasted for quite a few minutes. Then the sections closed up, and the whole thing started to sink, eventually disappearing beneath the waves.

One of the witnesses, the wife of another army officer, telephoned the Forte dos Andrades barracks at Guarajá, and the air force base was swiftly alerted. An aeroplane was sent as soon as possible to investigate, but it arrived on the scene after the objects had finally disappeared.

MUDDY WATERS

On 31 October 1963, eight-year-old Rute de Souza was playing near her home in Iguape, south-west of Santos, when she heard a roaring noise that was growing rapidly louder. Looking round, she saw a silvery object coming down out of the sky, heading towards a nearby river. After passing over the house, the UFO collided with the top of a palm tree and began to twist and wobble in the air. Then Rute saw it fall into the river, close to the far bank.

The child turned to run home, and met her mother who, alarmed by the noise, had been running towards the river. Then followed Rute's uncle, Raul de Souza, who had been working about 100 yards (90 metres) from the house. The three of them stood transfixed as they watched the surface of the river: at the spot where the object had sunk, the water was now seen to be 'boiling up'. This was followed by an eruption of muddy water, and then one of mud.

Rute was not the only witness. On the far bank, a number of fishermen had watched the spectacle. One of them, a Japanese named Tetsuo Ioshigawa, gave a detailed description of the incident to official investigators and reporters. The object, shaped like a 'wash basin', was estimated by him to have been about 25 feet (7.5 metres) in diameter; it had been no more than 20 feet (6 metres) off the ground when it hit the palm tree. The general assumption was that the object must have been in difficulties after the collision.

Some who had heard about the incident assumed that a wrecked 'flying saucer' was embedded in the muddy bottom of the river, but divers could find nothing in the 15 feet (5 metres) of water. Finally, engineers searched the area with the use of mine detectors; but they, too, failed to locate the object.

Speculating about the incident in the *Bulletin of the Aerial Phenomena Research Organisation* (APRO), Jim and Coral Lorenzon wrote that the reported size of the UFO suggested it could certainly have carried a crew. If so, then repairs may well have been effected that would have enabled the craft to escape.

THE UFO AT WAR

FLYING DISCS WERE BUILT BY THE NAZIS AND LATER BY SOME OF THE VICTORIOUS ALLIED POWERS. COULD SOME SIGHTINGS OF UFOS BE EXPLAINED BY SUCH UNCONVENTIONAL CRAFT?

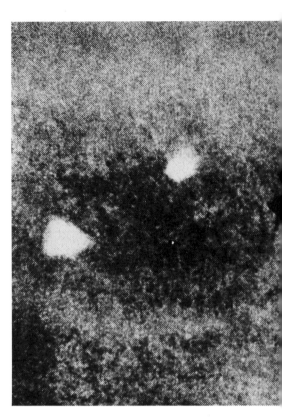

'The Nazis have thrown something new into the night skies over Germany. It is the weird, mysterious "foo fighter" balls which race alongside the wings of Beaufighters, flying intruder missions over Germany. Pilots have been encountering this eerie weapon for more than a month in their night flights. No one apparently knows what this sky weapon is. The "balls of fire" appear suddenly and accompany the planes for miles. They seem to be radio-controlled from the ground... '

The sightings referred to in this news story showed remarkable similarities. Lieutenant Schlueter of the 415th US Night Fighter Squadron, for example, reported being harassed by 'ten small balls of reddish fire' on the night of 23 November 1944 when flying over the Rhine; and pilots Henry Giblin and Walter Cleary reported that, on the night of 27 September 1944, they had been harassed in the vicinity of Speyer by 'an enormous burning light' that was flying above their aircraft at about 250 miles per hour (400 km/h). The mass of UFO reports agreed on two major points: the 'foo fighters' invariably appeared to ascend towards the aircraft from the ground; and they usually caused the aircraft's ignition systems to malfunction. Other reports, unconfirmed by the Allied forces, suggested that the malfunctioning of ignition systems had actually caused some aircraft to crash.

At first, the Allies thought that the 'foo fighters' were static electricity charges. But once this theory had been disproven, they then began to think that the balls of light were likely to be German or Japanese secret weapons, designed to upset the ignition systems of bombers. Another theory was

Canadian border over the Cascades, a mountain range in Washington State. There was much speculation that both the Soviets and the Americans, utilising men and materials taken from the captured secret research plants of Nazi Germany, were developing advanced disc-shaped aircraft.

FLYING PROTOTYPES

Speculation that there might be a connection between Nazi secret weapons and sightings of what seemed to be flying saucers increased when various West German newspapers and magazines began publishing articles during the mid-1950s about *Flugkapitan* Rudolph Schriever. According to these reports, this former Luftwaffe aeronautical engineer had designed, in the spring of 1941, the prototype for a 'flying top', which was test-flown in June 1942. With his colleagues Habermohl, Miethe and Bellonzo, he then went on to construct a larger version of the original 'flying disc' in the summer of 1944. At the BMW Plant near Prague, they then redesigned the larger model, replacing its former engines with advanced jets.

A brief description of Schriever's *Projekt Saucer* is given in Major Rudolf Lusar's book, *German Secret Weapons of the Second World War*.

'Habermohl and Schriever chose a wide-surface ring which rotated round a fixed, cupola-shaped

The rare photograph, above, shows 'foo fighters' – also known as 'kraut balls' – in company with Allied planes during the Second World War. Some aircrew described the mysterious spheres as being like silver Christmas tree decorations. The nickname came from the 'Smokey Stover' comic strip, popular at the time, in which the phrase 'where there's foo, there's fire' was often used.

The Chance-Vought Flying Flapjack, right, also known as the Navy Flounder, could take off nearly vertically and fly as slowly as 35 miles per hour (55 km/h), but was reported also to be capable of speeds greater than 400 miles per hour (640 km/h).

The Avro Car, left, was built for the US Air Force and Army by the Avro-Canada company, and was designed by an English engineer, John Frost. Officially, work on it was dropped in 1960, despite the early claim that the machine would reach twice the speed of sound.

that the objects had been designed purely for psychological warfare, and sent aloft to confuse and unnerve Allied pilots. Finally, both the RAF and the US Eighth Army, unable to solve the mystery, reached the conclusion that the 'foo fighters' were probably the product of 'mass hallucination'.

The 'foo fighters' disappeared from the skies a few weeks before the end of the war. Interestingly, the next wave of UFO sightings occurred in Western Europe and Scandinavia, between 1946 and 1948, when many people, including airline pilots and radar operatives, reported seeing strange cigar- or disc-shaped objects in the skies. There were sightings in the USA, too. On 21 June 1947, Harold Dahl reported seeing saucer-shaped objects flying towards the Canadian border. Three days later, Kenneth Arnold made his famous sighting of saucer-shaped objects also flying towards the

cockpit. The ring consisted of adjustable wing-discs which could be brought into an appropriate position for take-off or horizontal flight, respectively. Miethe developed a discus-shaped plate of a diameter of 42 metres [138 feet], in which adjustable jets were inserted.'

Other reports, which sometimes conflict in their details of the overall project, agree on the 'flying saucer's' size, and that it had a height from base to canopy of 105 feet (32 metres), reached an altitude of approximately 40,000 feet (12,000 metres) and attained a horizontal flight speed of 1,250 miles per hour (2,000 km/h).

Rudolph Schriever himself claimed, in the late 1950s, that he had indeed worked on a wartime research programme called *Projekt Saucer*. His 'flying disc' had been ready for testing in early 1945, but with the advance of the Allies into Germany,

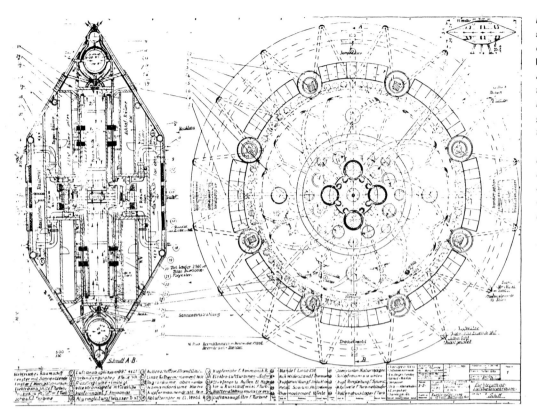

the test had been cancelled, the machine destroyed, and his complete papers mislaid or stolen in the chaos of the Nazi retreat.

Schriever died not long after these revelations, convinced to the end that UFO sightings since the end of the war were proof that his original ideas had been taken further with successful results.

But what were the 'foo fighters'? An identification was proposed by an Italian author, Renato Vesco, in a book first published in 1968. According to him the 'foo fighter' was actually the German *Feuerball* (Fireball), first constructed at an aeronautical establishment at Wiener Neustadt, Austria. The craft was a flat, circular flying machine, powered by a turbo-jet. It was used during the closing stages of the war, both as an anti-radar device and as a psychological weapon designed to disturb Allied pilots. Vesco says:

'The fiery halo around its perimeter – caused by a very rich fuel mixture – and the chemical additives that interrupted the flow of electricity by over-ionising the atmosphere in the vicinity of the plane, generally around the wing tips or tail surfaces,

// CHARLES ODOM, FORMER B-17

PILOT... SAYS THEY [FOO FIGHTERS]

LOOKED LIKE CRYSTAL BALLS,

CLEAR, ABOUT THE SIZE OF

BASKETBALLS, AND WERE OFTEN

SEEN OVER VIENNA, MUNICH AND

OTHER TARGET AREAS. **//**

HOUSTON POST, 7 JULY 1947

subjected the H$_2$S radar on the plane to the action of powerful electrostatic fields and electromagnetic impulses.'

Vesco also claims that the basic principles of the *Feuerball* were later applied to a much larger 'symmetrical circular aircraft', known as the *Kugelblitz* (literally, ball lightning), which could rise vertically by 'jet lift'.

Since neither the British, the Americans nor the Russians are ever likely to reveal what they discovered in the secret factories of Nazi Germany, it is worth noting that, in 1945, Sir Roy Feddon, leader of a technical mission to Germany for the British Ministry of Aircraft Production, reported:

'I have seen enough of their designs and production plans to realise that, if they had managed to prolong the war some months longer, we would have been confronted with a set of entirely new and deadly developments in air warfare.'

In 1956, Captain Edward J. Ruppelt, then head of the US Air Force's *Project Blue Book*, was able to state:

'When World War II ended, the Germans had several radical types of aircraft and guided missiles under development. The majority of these were in the most preliminary stages, but they were the only known craft that could even approach the performances of the objects reported by UFO observers.'

The first concrete evidence for post-war 'flying saucer' construction projects came in 1954. The Canadian government announced that the enormous UFO seen over Albuquerque, New Mexico, in 1951 was similar to a craft that they had tried to build shortly after the war. Owing to lack of adequate technology, however, they had eventually passed the design over to the United States.

Further evidence for United States' involvement with saucer-shaped aircraft projects was to be found in the US Navy's so-called *Flying Flapjack*.

The US soldier, above, guards a V-2 rocket, still lacking its outer skin. This vast underground factory at Nordhausen in Germany was top secret during the Second World War, along with many others whose secrets may still not have been revealed by the Allied governments.

Wernher von Braun, creator of the V-2, is seen, above right, with senior military staff at the Peenemünde range.

The *Flapjack,* also known as the *Navy Flounder,* was a circular aircraft, the design of which was begun during the Second World War. At that time, what the Navy needed was an aeroplane that could rise almost vertically so that it could take off from carriers, and could fly at just 35 miles per hour (55 km/h).

Little was known about that machine until early 1950, shortly after the US Air Force had ended its UFO investigation programme, *Project Grudge* (the forerunner of *Project Blue Book*). As part of an attempt to show that UFOs did not merit further investigation, the Air Force actually released a number of photographs and vague information about the *Flying Flapjack.*

Apparently, because the aircraft was wingless, reduced stability presented a problem. A later model, reportedly designated the XF-5-U-I, solved that problem.It was rumoured to be over 100 feet (30 metres) in diameter, and to have jet nozzles – resembling the 'glowing windows' seen on so many UFOs – arranged round its rim. It was built in three layers, the central layer being slightly larger than the other two. Since the saucer's velocity and manoeuvring abilities were controlled by the power and tilt of the separate jet nozzles, there were no ailerons (hinged flaps in the wings), rudders or other protruding surfaces. The machine was remarkably similar to those reported by UFO witnesses.

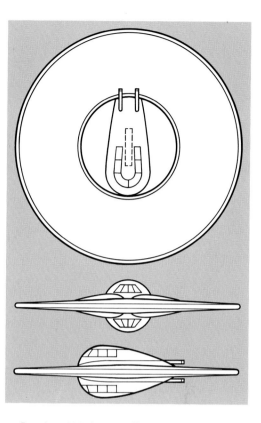

The flying disc, right, was designed by Dr Miethe, one of the team of brilliant engineers working on unconventional aircraft designs for the Nazi war effort. This 'saucer' was almost ready for operational use in 1945, when the factories in Prague were overrun by the Allies.

Research on saucer-shaped aircraft did not stop with the XF-5-U-I. On 11 February 1953, the *Toronto Star* reported that a new flying saucer was being developed at the Avro-Canada plant in Malton, Ontario. On 16 February, the Minister for Defence Production informed the Canadian House of Commons that Avro-Canada was working on a 'mock-up model' of a 'flying saucer', capable of flying at the remarkable speed of 1,500 miles per hour (2,400 km/h) and of climbing vertically. The president of Avro-Canada then wrote in *Avro News* that the prototype being built was so revolutionary that undoubtedly it would make all other forms of supersonic aircraft obsolete. The craft's official name was the *Avro Car.*

But, by 1960, it was officially claimed that the project had been dropped. The prototype of the Avro flying saucer is now in the US Air Force Museum in Fort Eustis, Virginia, and the Canadian and US governments have insisted that they are no longer involved with flying saucer construction projects.

Yet is this necessarily true? The possibility certainly remains that the Canadian, United States or Soviet governments could have continued to work on highly advanced, saucer-shaped, supersonic aircraft; and those directly involved in the projects, understanding the impossibility of testing the machines in complete secrecy, may well have opted for creating a smokescreen of confusion, rumour and systematic humiliation of UFO observers, thereby ensuring that they could fly their machines with impunity.

When one considers the extraordinary innovations of contemporary technology – jet aircraft, space rockets and reconnaissance satellites – and that what goes on behind the guarded fences of top-secret military and scientific establishments is probably decades ahead of these – then it becomes somewhat easier to give credit to the plausibility of such man-made saucers.

▟▟ Another theory is that the

foo-balls might have been a

type of plasma – in the form of

an electrical discharge –

known as St. Elmo's fire. ▟▟

Ronald D. Story,

UFOs and the Limits of Science

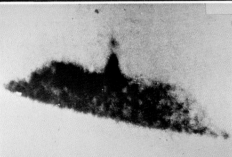

At about 7.45 p.m. on 11 May 1950 at his farm close by the Salmon River Highway, about 10 miles (17km) south-west of McMinnville, Oregon, Paul Trent and his wife claimed they saw a UFO. What is more, they took a remarkable photograph of it.

Mrs Trent was in the yard on the south side of the house, feeding the rabbits, when she saw, to the north-east, moving westwards, a disc-shaped object. She called her husband, who was inside the house. When he realised the unusual nature of the object in the sky, Paul Trent ran to his car for his camera, but his wife remembered that he had left it in the house and hurried to fetch it. It already contained a partly used film.

The object in the sky was tilted up a little as it approached, and appeared bright and silvery. It made no noise, and the Trents saw no smoke or vapour. Paul Trent took the picture, **top,** and wound on the film ready for the next frame, moving to the

right to keep the object in the view-finder, and taking a second shot some 30 seconds after the first. Mrs Trent said the object seemed to be gliding, with no rotating or undulating motion. It moved off westwards and 'dimly vanished', as she later put it.

The couple said there was a 'breeze' as the object tilted before flying overhead. The Trents estimated its diameter as 20-30 feet (6-9 metres).

A few days later, when he had used up the remaining frames, Paul Trent had the film developed locally. He did not seek publicity, telling his friends he wanted to avoid being 'in trouble with the government'. However, a reporter from the local **McMinnville Telephone Register** heard of the sighting from two of his friends; and, following it up, found the precious negatives on the floor of the Trents' house, under a writing desk where the Trent children had been playing with them! The **Telephone Register's** story appeared on 8 June 1950. On 9 and 10 June newspapers in Portland, Oregon and in Los Angeles ran the story, and **Life** magazine carried the photographs a week later.

None of this publicity had been sought by the Trents; and when, 17 years after the sighting, they were visited by an investigator from the US Air Force-sponsored Colorado University Commission of Enquiry (whose findings were later published as the **Condon Report**), he found them completely unchanged by their experience, well-liked locally and known as reliable.

The McMinnville UFO, **above left,** is remarkable for its similarity to an object, **above right,** seen and photographed from an aeroplane by a French Air Marshal near Rouen, France, in March 1954.

After submitting the photographs to rigorous scientific examination, the Condon investigation was forced to admit they might be genuine. The official report concluded:

'This is one of the few UFO reports in which all factors investigated, geometric, psychological and physical, appear to be consistent.'

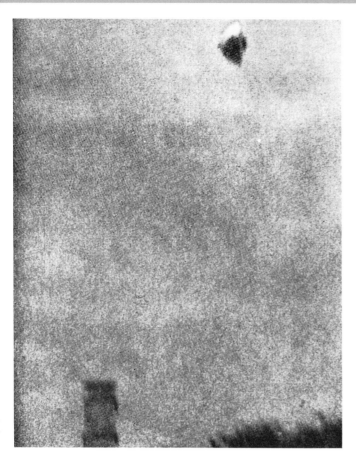

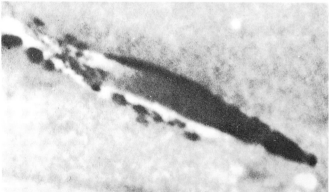

One warm, clear afternoon in early April 1966, an anonymous Australian was in his garden in Balwyn, near Melbourne, when it suddenly 'lit-up', and he saw in the sky a bright object, shaped like a mushroom, **left,** about 20-35 feet (6-10 metres) in diameter. It was about 150 feet (50 metres) from the ground and seemed to float down towards him, spinning through a 180° angle on its vertical axis, 'during which time I photographed it'. It then shot off northwards at high speed. A carpenter working in the house witnessed the object and also saw it being photographed.

The Australian is a qualified engineer, director of a large family business, and a respected citizen of Balwyn. It is difficult to believe he would perpetrate a hoax. But an American UFO organisation, Ground Saucer Watch Inc., of Phoenix, Arizona, has cast doubt on the authenticity of the photograph. Using computer techniques to analyse the photograph, GSW has claimed it is a fake. And yet GSW has been wrong in the past. The question as to who is correct in this instance thus remains unanswered.

A promotional photograph of a B-57 aeroplane in flight, **below,** found its way into a set of UFO photographs offered for sale by NICAP (National Investigation Committee on Aerial Phenomena). An unknown object appeared in the top right-hand corner of the photograph. According to UFO investigator Robert Schmidt, the object 'appeared to be streamlined, and to have dark "ports" on its lower periphery'.

Schmidt wrote to the manufacturers, the Martin Aircraft Company, asking for an enlargement, **inset left,** from the NICAP file. When questioned about the picture, the company replied that the unexplained image had been caused by a tear, a rub or an abrasion. Analysis, however, subsequently showed that, in the original negative, the emulsion grain extended over the area of the unknown object; a tear or rub would have destroyed the grain.

The Martin Company also said they had filmed another 'fly-by' to see if the same effect could be obtained again – a strange thing to do if, as they claimed, the original image had been caused by a flaw in the film.

AGENTS OF THE DARK

RARELY – IF EVER – DO THE THREATS OF THE MYSTERIOUS MEN IN BLACK, FOLLOWING A CLOSE ENCOUNTER, COME TO ANYTHING. SO WHAT COULD BE THE PURPOSE BEHIND THEIR VISITS?

In September 1976, Dr Herbert Hopkins, a 58-year-old doctor and hypnotist, was acting as consultant on an alleged UFO teleportation case in Maine, USA. One evening, when his wife and children had gone out leaving him alone, the telephone rang and a man identifying himself as vice-president of the New Jersey UFO Research Organisation asked if he might visit Dr Hopkins that evening to discuss certain details of the case. Dr Hopkins agreed: at the time, it seemed the natural thing to do. He went to the back door to switch on the light so that his visitor would be able to find his way from the parking lot, but while he was there, he noticed the man already climbing the porch steps. 'I saw no car, and even if he did have a car, he could not have possibly gotten to my house that quickly from any phone,' Hopkins later commented in delayed astonishment.

At the time, Dr Hopkins felt no particular surprise as he admitted his visitor. The man was dressed in a black suit, with black hat, tie and shoes, and a white shirt. 'I thought, he looks like an undertaker,' Hopkins later said. His clothes were immaculate – suit unwrinkled, trousers sharply creased. When he took off his hat, he revealed himself as completely hairless, not only bald but without eyebrows or eyelashes. His skin was dead white, his lips bright red. In the course of their conversation, he happened to brush his lips with his grey suede gloves, and the doctor was astonished to see that his lips were smeared and that the gloves were stained with lipstick!

An MIB visited Dr Herbert Hopkins and warned him to discontinue his investigations into an alleged UFO teleportation case on which he was working at the time. Taking a coin from Dr Hopkins, as illustrated above, the MIB promptly made it disappear, remarking that neither Hopkins nor anyone else on this plane would ever see that coin again.

It was only afterwards, however, that Dr Hopkins reflected further on the strangeness of his visitor's appearance and behaviour. Particularly odd was the fact that his visitor stated that his host had two coins in his pocket. It was indeed the case. He then asked the doctor to put one of the coins in his hand and to watch the coin, not himself. As Hopkins watched, the coin seemed to go out of focus, and then gradually vanished. 'Neither you nor anyone else on this plane will ever see that coin again,' the visitor told him. After talking a little while longer on general UFO topics, Dr Hopkins suddenly noticed that the visitor's speech was slowing down. The man then rose unsteadily to his feet and said, very slowly: 'My energy is running low – must go now – goodbye.' He walked falteringly to the door and descended the outside steps uncertainly, one at a time. Dr Hopkins saw a bright light shining in the driveway, bluish-white and distinctly brighter than a normal car lamp. At the time, however, he assumed it must be the stranger's car, although he neither saw nor heard it.

MYSTERIOUS MARKS

Later, when Dr Hopkins' family had returned, they examined the driveway and found marks that could not have been made by a car because they were in the centre of the driveway, where the wheels could not have been. But the next day, although the driveway had not been used in the meantime, the marks had vanished.

Dr Hopkins was very much shaken by the visit, particularly when he reflected on the extraordinary character of the stranger's conduct. Not surprisingly, he was so scared that he willingly complied with his visitor's instruction, which was to erase the tapes of the hypnotic sessions he was conducting with regard to his current case, and to have nothing further to do with the investigation.

Subsequently, curious incidents continued to occur both in Dr Hopkins' household and in that of his eldest son. He presumed that there was some link with the extraordinary visit, but he never heard from his visitor again. As for the New Jersey UFO Research Organisation, no such institution exists.

Dr Hopkins' account is probably the most detailed we have of an MIB (Man in Black) visit, and confronts us with the problem at its most bizarre. First we must ask ourselves if a trained and respected doctor would invent so strange a tale, and if so, with what conceivable motive? Alternatively, could the entire episode have been a delusion, despite the tracks seen by other members of his family? Could the truth lie somewhere between reality and imagination? Could a real visitor, albeit an impostor making a false identity claim, have visited the doctor for some unknown reason of his own, somehow acting as a trigger for the doctor to invent a whole set of weird features?

In fact, what seems the *least* likely explanation is that the whole incident took place in the doctor's

CASEBOOK

THE ODD COUPLE

On 24 September 1976 – only a few days after Dr Herbert Hopkins' terrifying visit from an MIB – his daughter-in-law Maureen received a telephone call from a man who claimed to know her husband John, and who asked if he and a companion could come and visit them.

John met the man at a local fast-food restaurant, and brought him home with his companion, a woman. Both appeared to be in their mid-thirties, and wore curiously old-fashioned clothes. The woman looked particularly odd: when she stood up, it seemed that there was something wrong with the way that her legs joined her hips. Both strangers walked with very short steps, leaning forward as though frightened of falling.

They sat awkwardly together on a sofa while the man asked a number of detailed personal questions. Did John and Maureen watch television much? What did they read? And what did they talk about? All the while, the man was pawing and fondling his female companion, asking John if this was all right and whether he was doing it correctly.

John left the room for a moment, and the man tried to persuade Maureen to sit next to him. He also asked her 'how she was made', and whether she had any nude photographs.

Shortly afterwards, the woman stood up and announced that she wanted to leave. The man also stood, but made no move to go. He was between the woman and the door, and it seemed that the only way she could get to the door was by walking in a straight line, directly through him. Finally the woman turned to John and asked: 'Please move him; I can't move him myself.' Then, suddenly, the man left, followed by the woman, both walking in straight lines. They did not even say goodbye.

THE OZ FACTOR

TIMELESSNESS AND A FEELING OF DISLOCATION ARE OFTEN REPORTED AFTER CLOSE ENCOUNTERS WITH UNIDENTIFIED FLYING OBJECTS. WHAT IS IT THAT CAUSES THIS SENSE OF ALIENATION?

There is, indeed, a marked social dimension to the UFO enigma. The phenomenon is not a fixed thing: it changes with the times and, perhaps, has done so for centuries. The airship waves of the 1890s in the USA, and those in 1909 and 1913 in Britain, for instance, showed UFOs keeping one step ahead of current technology; and the apparent similarities between the ancient fairy lore of many cultures and modern UFO entity sightings is equally striking. Note also the way that aliens, according to contemporary witnesses, no longer come from the solar system but from other stars or even other galaxies, now that our space probes have shown no sign of advanced life on any of our sister worlds.

The influence of science-fiction movies is relevant, too. *The Day the Earth Stood Still*, for instance, used the motif of electromagnetic interference with vehicles, some time before claims of this effect had even arisen in UFO accounts.

It has also been realised that identified flying objects (IFOs) are of great significance. Since more

The nature of UFO sightings seems to change with the times. In the 1890s, airships, like the one above, were widely seen in California. Later, after films such as The Day the Earth Stood Still, *above right, made in 1951, aliens and other forms of spacecraft were more frequently reported.*

There has been serious study of the UFO phenomenon ever since 1947; but one of the most frequent criticisms made of ufology is that no progress whatsoever has been made during this time. We are no nearer a solution, it is sometimes said, than on the day when Kenneth Arnold first encountered a formation of discs over Mount Rainier in Washington State, USA, all those years ago. Such an attitude dismisses out of hand, however, many important discoveries.

We now realise, for instance, that there is not just one type of UFO phenomenon but two – at least. On the one hand, there are physical occurrences, involving energy behaving in poorly understood ways. These are called unidentified atmospheric phenomena, or UAPs: on the other, there is interaction with UFOs involving human beings.

than 90 per cent of reported UFOs are in fact identified, it was always foolish just to dismiss them. Indeed, now there has been closer study of intriguing IFO cases, in which witnesses were fooled, by such commonplace sights as the Moon, into believing they had witnessed a UFO.

Ufology is now diversifying into a variety of subdivisions; and the scientific study of UAPs may even become a field of research on its own. UAPs, however caused, seem to be amorphous balls of energy that emit broad–band radiation. They could perhaps be related to ball lightning, whatever atmospheric physicists eventually prove that to be. Indeed, ball lightning may be a sub–category of UAPs, rather than the reverse. Another important kind of UAP may be a piezoelectrical impulse squeezed from the ground into the atmosphere. These lightforms may or may not be proven to exist, but such theories are at least providing ufologists with testable hypotheses.

But whereas UAPs may be seen by a number of independent observers, UFOs are very often totally subjective, or else perceived only by a small number of witnesses who are associated with each other in some way and who occupy a small area. But there has been speculation – by, for example, researcher Dr Michael Persinger – that UAP events may account for the more mysterious UFO close encounters as well.

PSEUDO-MEMORIES

According to Persinger, radiation emitted by the UAP may interfere with the brain functioning of any percipient who is close enough to it – that is, within the phenomenon's 'sphere of influence'. This proximity triggers hallucinatory experiences, which also feature unconsciousness, trauma, time-loss and pseudo-memories of an alien encounter, which are personally relevant but individually variable. They are said to be stimulated by the interpretation of the event (and made in the seconds before the UAP/brain interaction takes place) in terms of a culturally conceived 'alien device'. Many years ago, the same phenomenon would have been culturally conceived as demonic, or as from the fairy realm, during the same moments of interaction.

Dr Alvin Lawson and William McCall have attempted to prove an origin for subjective interpretations in terms of repressed memories of the birth process. Some factor such as this, present in all cases, is certainly necessary to explain the otherwise puzzling threads that interlink stories of alien contact from so many different countries – for the UFO enigma is world-wide in extent and also highly consistent.

Such research may be all that is necessary to establish a basic understanding of the UFO enigma. However, many problems remain. Why is there frequently gross distortion of normal stimuli, precipitating extraordinary close encounters? Why does there appear to be a connection between close encounter witnesses and psychic phenomena? Why do close encounter witnesses often become 'repeaters', having frequent UFO contacts, often from childhood?

Such difficulties, among others, give one cause to speculate as to whether a better, all–embracing or even additional theory to encompass the remaining cases may still be necessary. One important clue regarding this may be the existence of the 'Oz factor'.

The Oz factor comprises a set of features that stand out among UFO close encounter reports. Individually, they have been recognised for several years, but nobody had sought to tie them together into a collective experience. The following typical quotations from close encounter witnesses sketch in the outline of the Oz factor. 'All sounds around me suddenly ceased . . . it was like being at the bottom of a very deep well.' 'I felt isolated and alone, suddenly not a part of the environment.' 'It was as if I were half in this world and half out of it.' 'Time

In the film The Wizard of Oz, Dorothy and her dog Toto, seen bottom in a scene with the scarecrow, were transported out of their everyday life by a whirlwind. Those who have encounters with UFOs likewise often feel sucked into a void – hence the term 'Oz factor'.

> **"** I HAVE SPOKEN TO NUMEROUS WITNESSES... WHO TOLD ME THEY HAD BEEN CAUGHT IN A WHIRLWIND, HAD SEEN STRANGE CREATURES, AND HAD BEEN LEFT WONDERING AND CONFUSED... ALL I COULD OFFER THEM WAS THE ASSURANCE THAT THEY WERE NOT ALONE, THAT MANY OTHERS SHARED THE SAME EXPERIENCE, AND THAT I BELIEVED FUTURE SCIENCE WOULD EVENTUALLY ACCEPT AND UNDERSTAND IT AS AN IMPORTANT SOURCE OF NEW KNOWLEDGE. **"**
> **JACQUES VALLEE, DIMENSIONS**

seemed to slow down and then stand still. As this thing passed over, it literally took ages to do so.'

Essentially the Oz factor is a sense of timelessness and sensory isolation: the witness feels as if the UFO has temporarily sucked him out of the real world and into a kind of void where only he and the phenomenon co-exist. The name was given by analogy with the experience of Dorothy and Toto who, in *The Wizard of Oz,* were taken by a whirlwind to the land of Oz. The extent of this experience in the UFO records makes its importance obvious, for it is not something that investigators generally seek out. Rather, as a rule, it is reported spontaneously.

Often, a witness will come out of an encounter suffering considerable confusion about the length of time it has lasted. Indeed, it seems perfectly reasonable to suggest that cases of time-loss or time-lapse in contacts and abductions are the result of the Oz factor. This might very well suggest that many close encounters (possibly all) involve some degree of the Oz factor. After all, a time-loss of three or four minutes during a typical UFO experience could easily go unnoticed.

Memories retrieved hypnotically from time-loss cases seem to imply that some kind of 'message transfer' takes place during the 'lost' time. There is a disturbing consequence to be drawn from all this. A message transfer might indeed be present in all UFO close encounters, with the encounter itself being a mere side-effect. But in the majority of instances, this transfer, if it does take place, is never even suspected by the witness: it takes place beyond his normal conscious awareness.

SHARED EXPERIENCES

The existence of the Oz factor certainly points towards the consciousness of the witness as the focal point of the UFO encounter, for it is clearly here that the effects take place, whatever their cause may be. That this is so receives further vindication from an unexpected source, for the Oz factor, it seems, is not confined to UFO cases. Consider this description: 'I got this cold feeling . . . and I raised myself on my elbow. I could not hear the clock ticking and it was only a foot away from me. Everything was – how should I explain it? – like everything had stood still.'

This account comes from a witness about to see a ghost and evidently involves something akin to the Oz factor. Similar features have also been detected in out-of-the-body experiences, timeslips and precognitive visions. As the only obvious common denominator between all of these things is the mind of the percipient, suspicion must be directed

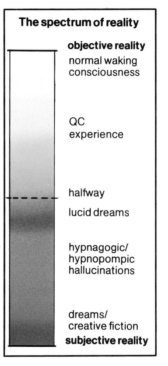

The spectrum of reality

objective reality
normal waking consciousness

QC experience

halfway
lucid dreams

hypnagogic/ hypnopompic hallucinations

dreams/ creative fiction
subjective reality

On the reality spectrum, **above,** *QC (quasi-conscious) experiences lie on the upper half of the scale between objective and subjective reality. Close encounters, out-of-the-body experiences, timeslips and precognitive visions all appear to be quasi-conscious experiences.*

> " UFONAUTS MAY EXISTS LARGELY IN THE EYE OF THE BEHOLDER. AFTER ALL, THE UFOS THEMSELVES MAY BE PLASMIC GLOBULES OF PURE INTELLIGENCE, AND THE UFONAUTS MAY BE NOTHING MORE THAN EXTERNALISED MENTAL PROJECTIONS RATHER THAN THE INDEPENDENT PILOTS THEY APPEAR TO BE. "
>
> **BRAD STEIGER,**
> **MYSTERIES OF TIME AND SPACE**

American airline pilot Captain E. J. Smith, right, *uses a dinner plate to illustrate the flying saucers he saw on 6 July 1947 over Oregon, USA.*

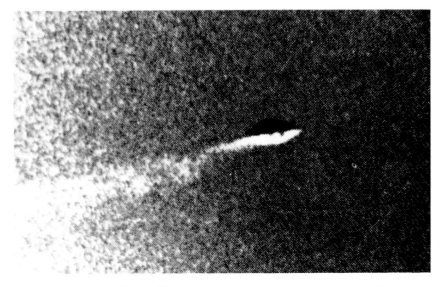

at consciousness once again. This is the stage on which the events are acted out.

Close encounters and many paranormal phenomena do indeed seem to have correspondences, if not necessarily exactly the same origin, so a general name is required for them. The term 'quasi-conscious experience' (or QC experience) has been adopted, as these events certainly come in the guise of normal reality and yet, in some ways, are very clearly not this.

A number of researchers, such as Patrick Austin and Hilary Evans, have suggested that we need a 'spectrum' to describe various facets of reality, and a development of this idea has proved invaluable in this connection. What we might call the 'spectrum of reality' would stretch from totally subjective experiences, such as dreams, to totally objective experiences, such as everyday waking consciousness. Both these extremes are, in fact, subject to

'interference' from other parts of the spectrum. For example, objective environmental factors, such as a cold breeze or loud noise, may affect a sleeper and make an appearance in another form in the subjective world of his dreams. The gulf between the two ends of the spectrum is far from empty. Lucid dreams, in which the dreamer is aware that he is dreaming and maintains some degree of control over dream imagery, seem to locate themselves towards the subjective end of the spectrum, but closer to the middle than the ordinary dream. Other phenomena, such as hypnagogic and hypnopompic hallucinations (the vivid images seen on the brink of sleeping and waking), also require to be placed towards the subjective end of the spectrum.

The QC experience fills what is otherwise a somewhat disconcerting gap on the spectrum between the middle and the objective end. Had we not known of it, we might have been tempted to invent it to prevent a lack of balance. The QC experience may even occupy quite a broad band of the spectrum not just a narrow one – but it is best appreciated as a kind of mirror image of the lucid dream. Whereas, in a lucid dream, objective information coming in from outside manipulates subjective dream reality, in the QC experience the reverse occurs: the subjective information manipulates what is experienced as objective reality.

This need not be seen as mind literally altering matter (although it remains an interesting possibility in view of quantum physics and brain/mind psychology, both of which may in some circumstances permit reality to be what our consciousness decides it to be). Possibly, in very rare instances, reality is manipulated sufficiently strongly to allow a photograph to be taken revealing the fact – and this may account for the few seemingly unimpeachable shots of UFOs. Usually, the manipulation of reality is not external, in the sense that it is visible to others or could be photographed, but takes place within the sensory systems of the percipient. What we perceive of the outside world is largely what our brain interprets from incoming signals. That is why optical illusions occur, and continue to occur, even when we know we are being fooled. And so, under the influence of a QC experience, our eyes might 'see' the Moon but our mind might 'experience' a UFO close encounter. Subjective information from some source has over-ridden the perception of objective reality to create the distortion – hence the very puzzling IFO cases. The overwhelming majority of close encounters might, on this basis, be reducible to ordinary stimuli seen 'under the influence', as it were.

Obviously, much work needs to be done to make progress with such hypotheses. But if they are in any way correct, we need to explore the origin of the subjective data that over-rides objective reality. It could be internal (from a deeper level of ourselves) or external (for example, from some other intelligence). It may even be both.

COSMIC CHAT SHOWS

If alien intelligence does exist, it is most unlikely to use primitive technology – radio telescopes, for instance. The intelligence may not have eyes or ears, for example. But consciousness itself may be the true radio telescope of the cosmos. On this basis, mind-to-mind chat shows may be going on around us all the time, while we search forlornly with our multi-million-dollar radio telescope toys. Only a few people (the psychic repeater witnesses, perhaps) may have sufficient receptiveness to 'tune in' to such cosmic conversations. If we did pick up such messages, our minds might be forced to replay them in terms of ideograms from our memory store (based on cliché interpretations of science fiction films and little green men). Each individual may produce a different picture, based on his personal image store, but there would be an essential similarity, since our views of images fitting the concept 'alien' are likely to be similar. Since this kind of 'similar but different' pattern is just what we find within UFO data, the theory may have some merit, despite its admittedly speculative nature.

Ever since that classic sighting by Kenneth Arnold, ufologists' own findings have been gradually eroding the 'extra-terrestrial hypothesis' in its usual form – the theory that UFOs are spaceships. The odd thing is that, now that we have found a number of mechanisms that seem to explain at least some aspects of the enigma in rational terms, we may be heading back full circle to a new but very different alien hypothesis: that UFOs are associated with alien consciousness making contact by way of the human mind.

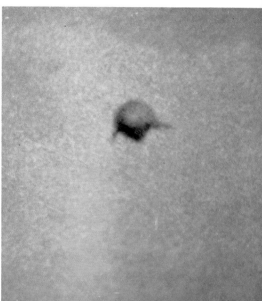

One of the two photographs taken of a daylight disc by a Mr Smith in Calgary, Canada, on 3 July 1967, is shown **left.** Both photographs were analysed by Ground Saucer Watch (GSW) but some time apart. The first photograph passed the tests with flying colours and was publicly announced to be 'genuine'. However, on analysing the second, GSW concluded that the film 'depicts the crudest attempt at a hoax that we have ever seen'. This contradictory analysis illustrates the limitations of GSW's computer analysis technique at the time.

The photograph, **below,** of what appears to be 'a slow moving fireball' was taken in Piedmont, Missouri, USA, on 22 March 1973. There was no known conventional or astronomical explanation for the sighting.

The airship-shaped object, **left,** was photographed near the small colonial town of Cocoyoc, south-east of Cuernavaca, Mexico, on 3 November 1973. Witnesses noted that it was about 30 feet (10 metres) across and Ground Saucer Watch concluded that the UFO must have been a military 'drone', used for meteorological purposes. Most people are unfamiliar with modern military hardware, which frequently results in mistaken reports of UFO sightings.

The disc-shaped UFO, **right,** photographed high over Namur, Belgium, on 5 June 1955, moved erratically and emitted a vapour trail.

Photographer Bill Burson caught the phenomenon, **below** – a bright streak – as it hovered over Pelham, Georgia, USA, on the night of 31 August 1973. The other streaks are stars, the effect being caused by the movement of the Earth during the photographic exposure. Although many explanations were put forward, the object that caused the large streaking remains unidentified. There were many witnesses, including several police officers of the South Georgia cities over which it was seen.

The daylight disc, **above,** was photographed by W.N. Henry during mid-August 1978 over the Dolomite Mountains, Italy. Henry, a New Zealander on holiday in Europe, had been involved in the photographic field for eight years and, although intrigued by the object – which he described as being silver and spherical – he thought it might have been a hot air balloon. Yet, as in the case of so many UFO pictures, the object was not seen by Henry when he took the photograph.

UFOs AND THE DIGITAL COMPUTER

COMPUTER PROCESSING OF PHOTOGRAPHS OF UFOS OFTEN CREATES STRIKING AND BIZARRE IMAGES, WHILE REVEALING SUBTLETIES THAT ARE DIFFICULT TO DISCERN IN THE ORIGINALS

The swirl of vivid hues, **top,** *is a 'computer eye view' of the photograph of a glowing disc seen over Colorado, USA,* **inset.** *The colours represent different brightness levels in the original image. The lines on the coloured image are drawn by the computer as it makes a number of measurements.*

Most photographs of unidentified flying objects are disappointing. They are blurred, lacking in detail and uninformative at a casual glance. Often, too, they lack the context of landscape that would enable us to judge the size and distance of the UFOs. Usually, too, any that are sharp and clear turn out to be fakes.

It is the task of the UFO photo analyst to sift through such low-grade material, to weed out the frauds and the misidentified aircraft, birds and astronomical objects, and to call attention to any residue of photographs that resist all attempts at being explained away.

Traditionally, UFO photo analysts have been limited to a few techniques of study. By measuring shadows, they may be able to show that a fake picture consists of a landscape shot combined with a picture of a model taken under totally different lighting conditions. By studying the focus on the UFO, they may also be able to show that it was much closer to the camera than the witness claimed, and was therefore much smaller than it appears. By enlarging details, the presence of any tell-tale trade mark can also be revealed. More frequently, we can identify the shot as showing some natural object – even the sceptics' favourite, the planet Venus, seen under unusual atmospheric conditions.

But, all too often, the label 'unidentified' has remained on a photograph because there was apparently too little information to resolve the question: 'What is this mysterious object in the sky?' Yet even in the fuzziest photograph, there are many subtle clues hidden away. Now, a powerful new tool, the computer, promises to disclose them.

One UFO investigation group, Ground Saucer Watch, has applied the computer to the analysis of UFO photographs on a large scale. Ground Saucer Watch was founded in Cleveland, Ohio, USA, in 1957 in order to bring a high level of technical expertise to the study of UFO reports. The group wanted, in the words of a statement made then, to 'see positive scientific action taken to end the elements of foul-up and cover-up in UFO research'. A large network of scientific and engineering consultants assists it in this task.

The computer has proved itself invaluable as an aid. It has enabled Ground Saucer Watch, for instance, in a study of 1,000 photographs that had *prima facie* plausibility, to reject all but 45 as misidentifications or hoaxes. The techniques used to sift such quantities of material are fascinating.

Pictures may be analysed with a so-called Computer Eye that uses a television-type camera to scan a picture and break it down into nearly a quarter of a million tiny 'pixels' (picture cells), in an array that comprises 512 columns and 480 rows.

Although the colours of the photographs provide important information, they do not necessarily come into such computer analyses. The scanner measures the brightness of each pixel and assigns it a rating on a 'grey scale' from 0 (completely dark) to 31 (bright white). So the whole picture is reduced to a quarter of a million numbers, which are stored in the computer's memory. They can be recalled and used to build up a black and white image, a direct copy of the original, on a television screen linked to the computer. But they can also be manipulated in countless different ways to generate new images, which may reveal the presence of unsuspected information in the original picture, or display it in unfamiliar and striking ways.

At the touch of a button, the computer operator can do most of the things that a photo technician can do only at the cost of several hours' work in his

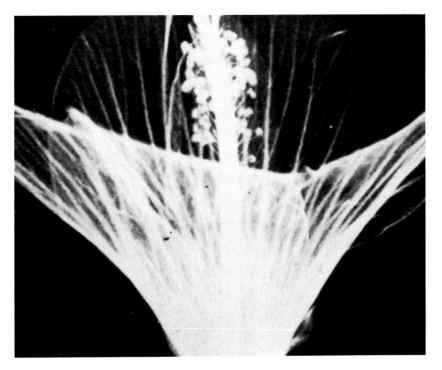

In the X-ray photograph of a flower, above, lighter areas represent thicker tissues which absorb X-rays more strongly than the thinner areas.

The computer processed version of the picture, below, shows edges separating light and dark areas that have been enhanced. UFO pictures can be similarly clarified.

laboratory. He or she can, for instance, instantly enlarge any selected detail of the picture to full-screen size. But there are limits to the degree to which this can usefully be done. The picture becomes coarser as the mosaic of pixels becomes more evident. This begins to happen when the picture has been enlarged by about four times, in height and breadth.

The computer can also 'stretch' the contrast, brightening the light areas and darkening the shadows, thereby emphasising the detail in a murky original. (This is what you do to your television picture when you turn up the contrast control.)

ENHANCING THE IMAGE
Measurements of distances and angles on the image become extremely easy with the aid of a computer. Crossed lines can be superimposed on the picture and moved at will, in order to identify points of interest The computer can then measure the positions of those points and instantly calculate distance and angles.

All this makes life easier for photo analysts, and enables them to plough through much more material than they could cope with otherwise. But the computer can also easily accomplish a number of feats that are impracticable, or even impossible, for the photo technician to perform.

It can, for example, enhance the edges of the features seen in a photograph. This effect is illustrated on this page with a picture that is a little more conventional than a UFO photo. The X-ray picture is of a flower and is in black and white. Each shade of grey carries information about the flower's thickness, and hence its ability to absorb X-rays at that point. In this negative image, the brighter areas correspond to thicker areas of plant tissue. There is a great deal of delicate structure to be seen in the petals and the central pistil.

But the eye's ability to distinguish shades of grey is limited. The result obtained when the edges are enhanced is also shown on this page.

Areas of uniform shade in the original are represented as a medium grey in the computer-processed picture. Wherever the original increases in lightness (from left to right), the computer draws a bright line; while where there is a transition from light to dark, it draws a dark line. The result is arresting. The flower's structure, which was lost in the subtle, veil-like X-ray image, is now laid bare in a tracery of metallic clarity.

Edge enhancement has little relevance to the indistinct forms visible in many UFO pictures. However, it is revealing when applied to UFO images showing faint detail. These are generally dark objects seen against the daytime sky. But another technique, colour coding, can extract information from the brightness pattern in the original pictures. This exploits the fact that the eye can distinguish colours far more readily than it can distinguish shades of grey.

In order to colour-code a picture, the computer is linked to a colour television set. Each pixel is then assigned a colour according to its brightness. Thus, in the X-ray picture of the flower, the darkest areas are shown as black. The darkest shades of grey (the

Like an artist with a taste for poster paints, the computer has transformed the X-ray flower picture on the previous page into a bold pattern of colours, below. All the detail is present in the original picture but is now presented in a form more easily 'read' by the human eye and brain.

thinnest parts of the flower) are rendered as shades of violet and red. Increasingly light areas are shown as shades of yellow, green and blue. The lightest areas (the thickest parts of the plant) are rendered as white.

The resulting picture is of a gaudier flower than nature ever created, with all the details of structure leaping out at the eye. Radiographers also use this type of colour coding on X-ray pictures to improve their view of the interior of the human body.

Astronomers and space engineers apply a similar technique to the pictures they take with ground-based telescopes, and to the television images sent back from space satellites and probes. In the original pictures, brightness levels may represent the actual brightness of a planet's surface, or the temperature of a gas cloud in space, or the intensity of radio waves from distant galaxies. The patterns in the computer-generated image will represent this information in terms of colour.

AN AMBIGUOUS MESSAGE

What, then, can the procedure reveal specifically about UFOs? The brightness pattern of light and dark in the image of a UFO is a complex and ambiguous 'message', involving the shape of the object, the amount of light it may be emitting at each point, its intrinsic lightness or darkness, if it is being seen by reflected light, the effects of glare and atmospheric haze, and so on. Emphasizing the pattern by means of a colour-coding technique often reveals the true nature of the object immediately. A broken, uneven density may indicate a cloud. A cylindrical shape with protuberances may appear, indicating an aircraft body and wings partly hidden by glare. Alternatively, the contours of a 'daylight disc' (meaning any daytime UFO) may be revealed, and often turn out to be suspiciously like those of a camera lens cap, a pie plate, or a hub cap.

Ground Saucer Watch has employed these techniques on thousands of photographs. Take, as an example, the two famous 'Colorado pictures', shown opposite. They indicate a single UFO, sighted and photographed at precisely 6.20 a.m. local time on 28 August 1969 by Norman Vedaa and his passenger while driving north-east on State Route 80S, approximately 70 miles (110 kilometres) from Denver, Colorado. Vedaa described the object as yellow-gold, tremendously brilliant, oval in shape, and soundless. He said: 'The object was bright, hard to look at – and appeared to hover momentarily. The object's glow. . . was producing a reflective light on – the clouds below... ' Two colour transparencies were taken and do indeed show a bright yellowish glow with well-defined edges, back-lighting the clouds.

The colour-coding technique was used on the Colorado photographs, and the result is reproduced on the first page of this feature. Again, lighter parts of the original are represented by white, blue and yellow, while darker parts are represented by red, violet and black.

The light vertical lines in that picture, and in the one below, shows different ways of displaying brightness information. The computer has taken a 'slice' down the picture along the left-hand line. At the right, it has plotted a graph of the brightness of the scene along that line, shown by the fluctuating

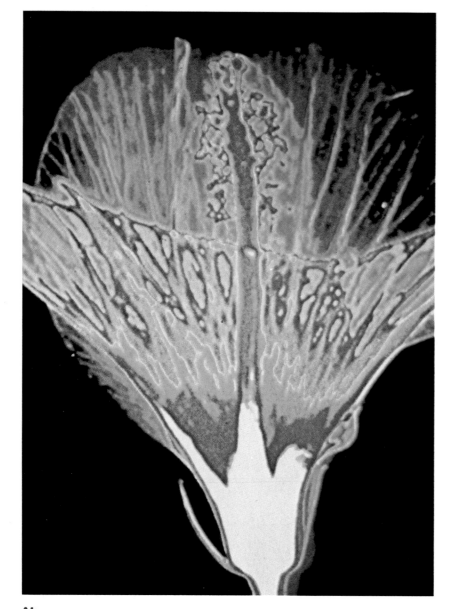

line. Thus, the 'bump' in the wavy line represents the bright centre of the object.

The computer can also speed up detailed study of light and shadow at any selected region of the picture. Ground Saucer Watch has a 'library' of data on the proportion of light that is reflected by each of a large range of materials. In some photographs of UFOS seen by reflected daylight, everyday objects, such as trees or houses, are visible, and the UFO image can be compared with them. This may enable the analyst to make a tentative judgement about the composition of the UFO.

Sometimes, the image of a UFO in the sky is beautifully sharp, while all ground features more than 50 feet (15 metres) away are slightly out of focus. This shows that the object is close to the camera – and so must be a fake (or have been piloted by very little green men).

In its study of the Vedaa pictures, Ground Saucer Watch has been able to rule out more and more explanations that seek to reduce the sightings to causes that are well-known and understood. This was no weather balloon, flock of birds or daylight meteor – the brightness distribution was that of a disc. It was not an aircraft hidden in the glare of reflected sunlight – it was too bright for that, and not a trace of tail or wings could be found. Lens flares, reflections from clouds, mirages and other atmospheric effects are all ruled out: the Sun is in the wrong position for them.

In the near future, photo analysis is likely to be carried out by even more sophisticated computers, working with scanners that can break down the original image into yet finer detail. Soon, it will become virtually impossible to fake a UFO photograph. Then, perhaps, the matter will be solved.

American motorist, Norman Vedaa, saw a brilliant disc and stopped his car to photograph it. It is visible near the upper centre of the picture, **top.** *The second picture,* **above,** *was taken within a few seconds and was the original of the processed UFO images on the first page of this article. The disc flew off at high speed.*

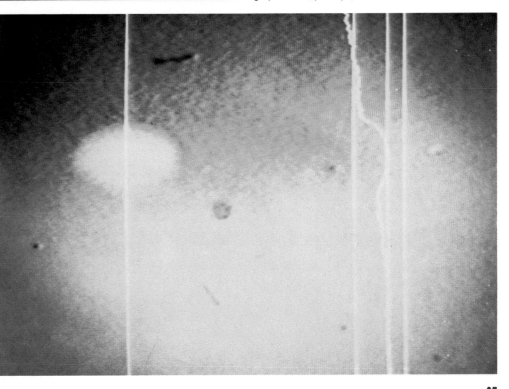

Measurements of image brightness can be made by computer, as shown **right.** *The measurements are made along the left-hand line. The fluctuating line curves to the right where the photograph is brightest. This curve helped to prove the disc was not a lens flare, weather balloon or aircraft.*

UFO WATCHING

THERE ARE SEVERAL EMINENT RESEARCHERS WHO HAVE DEVOTED MUCH TIME AND ENERGY TO LOOKING INTO THE NATURE OF UFO SIGHTINGS. WHEN, FOR INSTANCE, HARLEY RUTLEDGE SET OUT ON A ROUTINE UFO INVESTIGATION, HE DID NOT RECKON ON IT TAKING SEVEN YEARS. NOR WAS HE TO KNOW THAT HIS FINAL REPORT WOULD BE A MAJOR LANDMARK IN UFO RESEARCH

It was phenomena such as those in the sky at night over Piedmont, below, and Cape Girardeau, bottom, that started Harley Rutledge on his studies. Researchers had grown disenchanted with lights in the sky as evidence of UFO activity, since such sightings were open to many interpretations. But Rutledge's Project Investigation was to use monitoring techniques to prove that images, like the two shown here, were very definitely not the product of natural phenomena.

Practical ufology is, for many, a contradiction in terms. Indeed, faced with the elusive and often paradoxical nature of all the evidence that has been put forward by witnesses to date, a number of ufologists have reached the conclusion that there is no possible material explanation for the phenomenon.

But French-born ufologist Jacques Vallee is just one of a growing number of more advanced researchers who consider that the subject is, in fact, of a much more complex nature. As he declared in a paper delivered to the American Institute of Aeronautics and Astronautics: 'The UFO phenomenon is the product of a technology that integrates physical and psychic phenomena.' If this is so, then, since orthodox science is better equipped to cope with physical rather than with psychic material by way of evidence, it might well be best to concentrate primarily on investigating the material aspect of UFO sightings.

It was in just such a matter-of-fact frame of mind that Harley Rutledge embarked on what probably ranks as the most important piece of practical ufology yet carried out. It began in 1973 when, as professor of physics at South-East Missouri State University at Cape Girardeau, he was confronted with an intriguing challenge. Near the town of Piedmont, some 50 miles (80 kilometres) from

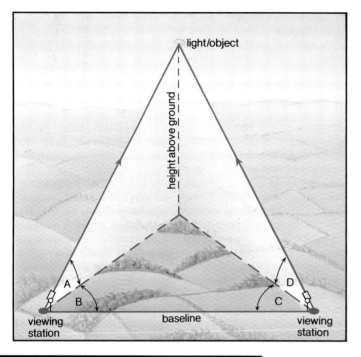

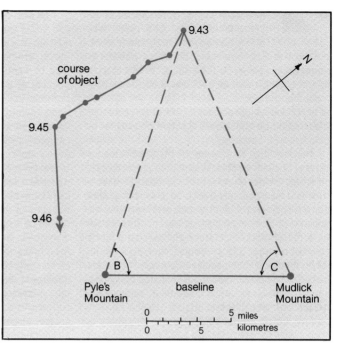

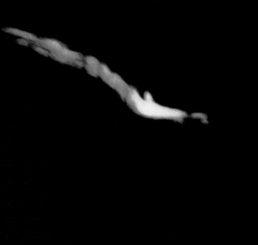

Cape Girardeau, curious lights had been seen on numerous occasions by many witnesses, in circumstances that seemed to defy any conventional explanation. As a scientist, Rutledge accepted the challenge to explain the phenomena, collecting together a team of specialists in various fields, gathering whatever monitoring and recording instruments he could find, and setting off for the site in the expectation that two or three weekends of expert observation should suffice.

But it was not until seven years later that his report on the investigation was published – the result of nearly 2,000 man-hours of observation by Rutledge and his team of colleagues. During that period, they observed 178 UFOs, 157 of which were recorded on their monitoring instruments, and combined visual observation and photographic records with radar and other forms of detection that were set up in separate locations for simultaneous monitoring.

The great majority of the phenomena observed by Rutledge's team took the form of lights in the sky, generally at night, with little or no discernible shape. This was unfortunate: there has been an

Principles of triangulation, as illustrated above left, can be used to plot an object's height and distance from the ground. To make the calculation, the vertical angles (A and D) and the horizontal angles (B and C) must be measured simultaneously from two points on the ground, a known distance apart (baseline).

The plan view, above right, is of the course of a UFO seen on 25 May 1973, as plotted by Project Investigation. At 9.43 p.m., researchers at the observation posts at Pyle's Mountain and Mudlick Mountain, 11 miles (18 kilometres) apart, had the object in view. Using triangulation, they were able to measure the height and the distance of the UFO and thereby pinpoint its position. Between 9.43 and 9.46, nine such points were located at 15-second intervals.

increasing tendency among ufologists to disregard this type of sighting unless there is very good circumstantial evidence surrounding it, because there is very little to be deduced from a blob of light. Besides, lights are the most easily misinterpreted of all visual phenomena: whereas a domed disc with portholes must be either a 'nuts and bolts' craft or an illusion of some kind, a light-blob can be anything from a car headlamp to a meteorite, a satellite or even light reflected off a flock of birds.

PRACTICAL APPROACH

However, Rutledge's highly practical approach, concerned only with the facts of the sightings, quickly eliminated any such obvious causes of misidentification. Using the surveyors' technique of triangulation, the precise location and course of the objects could be established and plotted, which meant that their size, altitude and speed could also be accurately established.

The following is a typical example of the observations made by Rutledge's team – a sighting recorded on 25 May 1973. That evening, two field units had been set up, one on Pyle's Mountain ('P') and the other on a fire tower on Mudlick Mountain ('M'), some 11 miles (18 kilometres) distant.

The two observation points were equipped with monitoring instruments, and were in radio contact with each other.

At 9.37 p.m., the four observers at P reported a light towards the west. The observers at M immediately confirmed this, and at once initiated the measuring of bearings and altitudes, which were transmitted every 15 seconds, and also recorded on video tape.

At 9.42, those at P reported the object as 'moving across the sky rather slowly; it is fairly bright, say a first-magnitude star. It is yellowish/orange in colour.' Those at M reported: 'We have it in full view now.'

By 9.43, with observers at both posts obtaining a clear view of the object, its precise location was calculated by triangulation. Between 9.43 and 9.46,

The four photographs on this page are stills that have been taken from a movie film made by an Associated Television camera team while working on the programme *Farming Today,* near Birmingham, England, in October 1972.

Cameraman Neil Stuart caught the brightly shining streak as it shot across the sky, *above.* It grew in length, as shown *above right* and *right,* and finally split into two barely visible 'blips', *below,* before vanishing.

The team reported the sighting to the authorities and to UFO investigators. Jenny Randles of Northern UFO Information Network watched the film and concluded that the 'UFO' was probably an F-111 tactical bomber from a nearby US Air Force base, jettisoning fuel. This was denied by a spokesman for the USAF – quite understandably, as offloading fuel is actually illegal over arable land. The case remains – rather unsatisfactorily – open to a number of interpretations.

The brilliant, gold-coloured UFO, *above,* was seen and photographed by Norman Vedaa and an anonymous friend near Denver, Colorado, USA, at 6.20 a.m. on 28 August 1969.

The solitary UFO was hovering over the highway when Vedaa saw it and grabbed his camera. He noted the object's 'extreme brilliance' and seemingly solid appearance, while his companion took the first of two photographs. They then drew in to the hard shoulder and took the second picture, remarking that the UFO was making no sound. While adjusting the camera, they saw, out of the corner of their eyes, the UFO turn and fly away at great speed, to 'disappear within seconds'. The pictures were subjected to the battery of computerised tests used by Ground Saucer Watch, Inc. These indicated that the object was dense, three-dimensional and distant from the camera – in short, a true UFO. GSW concluded: 'The images cannot be explained by any presently known natural or celestial phenomena.'

An alleged spacecraft is seen hovering over the Sixth Annual Spacecraft Convention, held at Giant Rock, in the Mojave desert, California, in the 1950s, *right.* That a UFO should put on such a display at such a gathering – and be photographed into the bargain – seems almost too good to be true. The most likely explanation is that the photograph in fact shows a 'dust devil', caused by a miniature whirlwind. But there is another possibility: that delegates to such a convention might, whether consciously or otherwise, wish to see a visiting alien spacecraft, projecting this wish on to the environment and thence on to film. If so, this is indeed a remarkable photograph.

THE LONG SHADOW OF FEAR

MEN IN BLACK EXCITED A GREAT DEAL OF ATTENTION WHEN THEY BEGAN TO THREATEN UFO WITNESSES IN THE 1950S. BUT THE POWERFUL SYMBOL OF THE SINISTER BLACK-CLAD FIGURE IS CENTURIES OLD

UFO percipients and investigators are by no means the only people to receive visits from Men in Black (MIBs). Researchers Kevin and Sue McClure, investigating the North Wales religious revival of 1905, found accounts that bear at least a *prima facie* similarity to the more recent MIB phenomenon:

'In the neighbourhood dwells an exceptionally intelligent young woman of the peasant class, whose bedroom has been visited three nights in succession at midnight by a man dressed in black. This figure has delivered a message to the girl which, however, she is forbidden to relate.'

The young woman in question (a farmer's wife-

Montague Summers (1880-1948), above, was a writer who traced a number of historical MIB cases – years before the first modern, UFO-related MIB encounter in 1953.

In The Last Judgement, below, *by Fra Angelico (c.1400-1455), the damned, seen on the right, are being dragged off to Hell by black demons. Some modern writers have gone as far as to suggest an identification between these sinister figures and MIBs.*

turned-preacher), Mary Jones, one of the leading figures of the religious revival, was well known for the mysterious lights that appeared as she pursued her mission. On one occasion, when she encountered her sinister visitor at night, Mary was 'rescued' by one of her lights, which darted a white ray at the apparition. The MIB promptly vanished.

It all sounds like the wildest fantasy – except that there is substantial evidence for some of the phenomena reported, many of which were seen by independent witnesses, some of them avowedly sceptical. But does this mean that the MIBs really existed, and actually appeared in the bedroom of that 'intelligent young woman of the peasant class'? What we are learning about the modern wave of MIBs may help us to understand similar cases reported in earlier periods.

Men in Black turn up, in one form or another, in the folklore of almost every country of the world, and periodically emerge from legend into everyday life. On 2 June 1603, a young country lad confessed, before a court in south-west France, to several acts of werewolfery, culminating in the kidnapping and eating of a child. He stated that he was acting under the orders of the Lord of the Forest, to whom he was bond-slave. He described the Lord of the Forest as a tall, dark man, dressed in black, and riding a black horse.

UNDER COVER OF DARKNESS

Montague Summers, who reports the case in his book *The Werewolf*, has no hesitation in identifying this, and all other MIBs, with the Devil of Christian teaching, and it continues to be a widespread interpretation. Even today, there are theorists who claim that UFOs are diabolical in origin, and that consequently the MIBs must be Satan's agents. In those parts of the world where the prevailing religious doctrine presupposes two warring factions of good and evil, good is equated with light and evil with darkness. The agents of good tend to be blond and dressed in white, while the agents of evil have dark hair and are dressed in black. Other connotations inevitably follow. Under cover of darkness, all kinds of tricks can be carried out and crimes committed.

Darkness is also associated with winter, and so with death: in almost all parts of the world, death rites and customs are also associated with the colour black.

So, whatever his specific role, the MIB is a distinctly sinister figure. He is a trickster, and he stands for lies rather than truth, death rather than life.

But because of the obviously symbolic elements involved, many theorists speculate that MIBs are not flesh-and-blood creatures at all, but mental constructs projected from the imagination of the percipient, and taking on a form that blends traditional legend with contemporary imagery. But it cannot be quite that simple: too many of the accounts show

Among many cultures, the colour black represents dark and sinister elements. The representation of the demon god Kal Bahairab from the Hanuman Doka temple in Nepal, below, shows him with a hideous face, four arms and black skin. Human beings were, in former times, sacrificed to this god to satisfy its lust for blood.

evidence of relating to physical creatures moving in the real, physical world.

There are several possible explanations. At their most concrete, the MIBs who visit today are supposed to be the representatives of an official department – sometimes as straightforward and above board as the Air Force, sometimes a more covert organisation, such as the CIA or FBI. The average American, in particular, seems far from convinced that investigative bodies, such as the CIA, are necessarily working in the public interest. The same attitude of mind that has evolved the conspiracy theories about UFOs – that a gigantic cover-up is being mounted by the government – suggests that the MIBs are part of this operation, their sole object being to conceal the facts by silencing witnesses and purloining photographs and other evidence of encounters with extra-terrestrials.

The fact that the identities of a great many MIBs have been checked, and that they have invariably been found not to be the persons they purport to be, lends strength to such suspicions, which can amount to virtual paranoia. In 1970, an American theorist, Tony Kimery, wrote in all seriousness:

'The mysterious MIBs and the entire collection of their thugs, henchmen, and highly trained

Richard Baxter, below, was a 17th-century writer who recounted the tale of a London woman of the time – a 'pious, credible woman' – who was encouraged to hang herself by the Devil in the shape of a big black man. The archetype of a black figure as a symbol of evil appears repeatedly in legend.

intelligence officers, are a big part of the complex UFO phenomena which is in turn part of another big and complex phenomena (*sic*). It is known that projects by them are now under way for the complete control of... political, financial, religious and scientific institutions. They – the MIBs – have a very long background and history that stretches back for centuries, indicating a massive build-up of concentration to where it is today.'

MYSTERIOUS ORIGINS

MIBs are often reported as being dark skinned, and having either a defective command of English, or conversely an over-precise way of talking that suggests that they are not speaking their own tongue. Mary Hyre, a West Virginia journalist, noted that a strange visitor picked up a ball-point pen from her desk and examined it with amazement, as if he had never seen anything like it before. And UFO percipient Mrs Ralph Butler, who received a visit from a man who claimed to be an Air Force major, was astonished to find that he was so unfamiliar with American food that he had to be shown how to eat it. The implication is that they are foreigners, an attitude encouraged by American xenophobia. Curiously, though, no witness appears to have suggested that the MIBs are of Russian origin.

Where specific details are mentioned, it is always implied that they are vaguely 'oriental'. Slanting eyes are frequently reported; and the deadpan faces suggest the supposedly inscrutable Asian. Sometimes, heads are totally bald. (By linking 'the yellow peril' with the 'man in black', of course, it is possible to frighten oneself with two bogeymen for the price of one!)

Although witnesses rarely state openly that they believe their visitors to come from beyond Earth, this is often clearly implied. The three men reported by Albert Bender of Bridgeport, Connecticut, USA, in 1953 – at the start of the modern MIB wave – were clearly of alien origin. Other MIBs have displayed behaviour traits that seem to suggest that they are able to function for only a limited timespan. After a while, they insist that they have to leave, or take pills, or drink water, and sometimes show signs of losing strength. A further possibility remains – that the MIBs are neither flesh-and-blood (even extra-terrestrial flesh-and-blood), nor some form of hallucination/illusion, but something in between. The entities encountered in a recent French case even seem to have existed, if 'existed' is the word, on some alternative plane of being.

The alleged abduction, in December 1979, of Franck Fontaine for seven days on board a UFO was one of the rare French cases to have attracted worldwide attention. The abduction itself was, of course, the central event of the case, but it was only the start of a series of incidents. One of these, involving MIBs, concerned another member of the trio, Jean-Pierre Prévost, who told this story:

'The night of Friday the seventh to Saturday the eighth of December 1979, Franck, Salomon and I had sat up talking for a long time, and went to bed sometime around 5 to 5.30 in the morning. At 7 a.m., there was a ring at the door. Salomon and Franck didn't hear it, so I went to open the door. I found myself in the presence of three fellows. One was of average height, very well dressed in dark green, almost black, black tie, white shirt, and waistcoat to match his suit; he had a fringe of beard, black like his hair, and a moustache. His general appearance was pretty good. The others were bigger than him, taller and more heavily built.

'What follows, I haven't told the police – I reported the visit itself to them – because we've already had enough of being taken for crackpots! But these two types, with the bearded man, didn't really exist, that I'm certain of! In the first place, they had no sight. That's hard to explain: they fixed me with their eyes, but those eyes were nothing but a white mass, all over. They were terrifying!

'The bearded fellow asked me: "Are you one of the three?" He obviously meant, was I one of the three people concerned in the Ciergy-Pontoise case? I said yes, and he went on: "Good, in that case, you can pass the word to your companions: you've already said too much. An accident will happen to you. And if you say any more, it will be more serious than that...

'And, with that, they vanished; but how, that's something I can't begin to explain. They didn't take the lift, I'd have heard it if they did; and even more so if they'd used the stairs – the door makes a deafening row! I went to the window that overlooks the parking lot. I can tell you definitely that, all night, at least until 5 a.m. or later, we'd noticed a Ford Capri in metallic green standing beneath our window, a Ford that we didn't recognise. Well, when I looked down, there was this Ford, just starting up. How had they managed to get to it without using the stairs or the lift? Complete mystery.

'I woke up Franck and Salomon and we went to the police, without giving them the unbelievable details about the two toughs. The police said: "So long as they didn't actually attack or wound you, there's nothing we can do, so get back home." And that was that.'

FORCES OF EVIL

Jean-Pierre told investigators that he saw the three men on several subsequent occasions – either from across the street or at a market. On one occasion, he received another warning while he was in a tobacco store buying cigarettes. He was told to keep quiet about their experiences and was also threatened. Subsequently, under hypnosis, Jean-Pierre indicated that the entities were not extra-terrestrials but *intra-terrestrials*, forces of evil originating from inside the Earth. He also added – intriguingly – that the bearded man had been real, but that his two henchmen had been 'unreal'.

Cases such as this are made baffling by their inconsequentiality. But one thing seems certain: just as the MIB visits seem to originate from some psychic or mental link between the MIBs and the witness, so the consequences of the visit depend less on the MIBs than on the attitude adopted by the witness. If the percipient takes the MIBs at their face value, and believes their threats, he or she is liable to find himself heading for a breakdown. Paranoia may develop, and he may believe himself followed everywhere, harassed by paranormal happenings, such as strange telephone calls and poltergeist phenomena. It is possible that these second-stage phenomena are genuine as far as the

The three men, top – from left to right, Salomon N'Diaye, Jean-Pierre Prévost and Franck Fontaine – were involved in a famous case of alleged abduction by the UFO shown in the sketch, above. Prévost was later the victim of a threatening visit from MIBs.

victim himself is concerned. Although they are manifestations of fears, they are none the less real for that and will not disappear until he capitulates and gives up his UFO studies, if he is an investigator, or keeps quiet about what happened during his experiences, if he is a witness.

If, on the other hand, he braves the matter out – if he refuses to abandon his investigation, and continues to tell the world of his experiences – it seems the MIBs are powerless against him. Carlos de los Santos, stopped on his way to a television interview by a gang of tough, threatening characters, was momentarily scared; he turned his car round, went home and cancelled the interview. But a friend reassured him and persuaded him not to let himself be intimidated. A fortnight later, he gave the interview – and he heard nothing subsequently from the MIBs!

The MIB phenomenon is clearly worth studying carefully. Whatever the nature of the MIBs – whether they are wholly illusory, or whether there is a measure of reality in them – they exert a great deal of power over the minds of their victims. The better we understand them, the more we may learn about how such power may be deployed. If for no other reason, the MIB phenomenon is important because it gives the sociologist a chance to study a legend in the making. Indeed, the sinister MIB masquerade provides us with contemporary phenomena that rank with the witch, the vampire and the werewolf of times past.

"

I HAVE IN MY FILES HUNDREDS OF CASES... IN WHICH YOUNG MEN AND WOMEN OBSESSED WITH THE UFO PHENOMENON HAVE SUFFERED FRIGHTENING VISITS FROM THESE APPARITIONS...

"

JOHN A. KEEL,

UFOS – OPERATION TROJAN HORSE

MYSTERIOUS FLYING MACHINES

ventional aircraft. But when military spokesmen comment, they always exclude the possibility that they might be accurately perceived craft — aircraft of remarkable capabilities, intended to remain hidden from the eyes of the public.

Supposed UFO sightings of much earlier times might well have been due to natural phenomena of a kind that would have baffled and frightened people less technically developed than ourselves – phenomena such as comets, meteors, noctilucent clouds, ball lightning, mirages, and so forth. But there is considerable evidence to support the suggestion that recent waves of 'flying saucer' sightings may be based on a new factor – that of flying machines constructed here on Earth.

The first 'modern' UFO sightings were the 'mystery airships' seen by thousands of people all over the United States between November 1896 and May 1897. At that time, European inventors were far ahead of their American counterparts in airship experimentation, but neither the French nor the Germans had managed to design an airship that could do much more than hover. Not until 1904 was the first dirigible – Thomas Baldwin's *California Arrow* – flown, in Oakland, California. Consequently, the mystery airships of 1896 and 1897 were as inexplicable and frightening as are the UFOs of today.

Significantly, the mystery airships were invariably reported as being cylindrical or cigar-shaped, and driven by a motor attached to a propeller – in short, they were exactly like the forthcoming airships. They also seemed to be manned by human beings, not by creatures from another world. In

WERE THE STRANGE AIRSHIPS, SIGHTED IN HUGE NUMBERS IN THE 1890S, ALIEN CRAFT? OR WERE THEY PERHAPS CREATED BY HUMAN ENGINEERS, ADVANCED IN AERONAUTICS?

Explanations offered for unidentified flying objects have been numerous and varied. In past ages, they were at times regarded as supernatural visitants or omens, divine or demonic in origin. In our own technological age, they are sometimes thought to be visitors from distant civilisations in space, time-travellers, or even emissaries of dwellers inside the Earth. Those who despair of ever finding evidence for such conjectures speculate that UFOs might be 'thoughtforms', created by those who believe they perceive them, or that they could be the results of governmental mind manipulation. Scientific debunkers, meanwhile, insist that they are misinterpreted natural phenomena or con-

The non-rigid airship, above, was built by Santos-Dumont of France at the turn of the century. Nothing as advanced as this was publicly known in the USA.

An aerial object, seen over California in 1896, was portrayed in a local newspaper, as shown right. Witnesses saw a dark body above a brilliant light, apparently descending.

EN L'AN 2000

fact, their occupants were often reported to have talked to witnesses, usually asking them for water for their machines.

IN GREEN PASTURES

Perhaps the most intriguing of all such cases were those involving a man who called himself Wilson. The *Houston Post* of 21 April 1897 carried an account of an event that took place in Beaumont, Texas, two days previously, when J. B. Ligon, the local agent for Magnolia Brewery, and his son noticed lights in a neighbour's pasture a few hundred yards away. They went to investigate and came upon four men standing beside a 'large, dark object', which neither of the witnesses could see clearly. One of the men asked Ligon for a bucket of water. Ligon gave it to him and the man gave his name as Wilson. He then told Ligon that he and his friends were travelling in a flying machine, that they had taken a trip 'out of the Gulf' and that they were returning to the 'quiet Iowa town' where the airship, and four others like it, had been constructed. When asked, Wilson explained that the wings of the airship were powered by electricity. Then he and his friends got back into the passenger car at the bottom of the airship, and Ligon and his son watched it ascend and fly away.

The next day, 20 April, Sheriff H. W. Baylor of Uvalde, also in Texas, went to investigate a strange light, as well as voices behind his house. Here, he encountered an airship and three men. Again, one of the men gave his name as Wilson, and said he came from Goshen, New York State. Wilson then enquired about a certain C.C. Akers, former Sheriff of Zavalia County, saying that he had met him in Fort Worth in 1877 and now wanted to see him again. Sheriff Baylor, surprised, replied that Akers was now at Eagle Pass, 60 miles (96 kilometres) to the south-west. Wilson, apparently disappointed, asked to be remembered to him the next time

In 1900, the world's conception of air travel was still dominated by the image of the airship. In the illustration, top, *an artist imagines an aerial ironclad of the year 2000, suspended from a somewhat vulnerable gasbag and battling with aeroplanes and ships.*

One of Samuel Pierpont Langley's designs for a pilotless aeroplane, powered by a light petrol engine, is shown above. *Some of his small aircraft were successful; but in 1903, two of his full-scale planes crashed.*

Sheriff Baylor visited him. The men from the airship then asked for water and requested that their visit be kept a secret from the townsfolk. They now climbed into the passenger car of the airship, before its great wings and fans were set in motion. They then sped away northward in the direction of San Angelo. The county clerk also claimed to have seen the airship as it left the area.

Two days later, in Josserand, Texas, a whirring sound awakened a farmer, Frank Nichols, who looked out of his window and saw 'brilliant lights streaming from a ponderous vessel of strange proportions' in his cornfield. Nichols went outside to investigate; but before he reached the object, two men walked up to him and asked if they could have water from his well. Nichols agreed, and the men then invited him to view the airship. He said there must have been six or eight crew members. One of these told him that the ship's motive power was highly condensed electricity and that it was one of five that had recently been constructed in a small town in Iowa with the backing of a large company in New York.

The next day, 23 April, witnesses, described by the *Post* as 'two responsible men', reported that an airship had descended where they lived in Kountze, Texas, and that two of the occupants had given their names as Jackson and . . . Wilson.

On 27 April, the *Galveston Daily News* printed a letter from C.C. Akers, who claimed that he had indeed known a man in Fort Worth named Wilson, that Wilson was from New York, and that he was 'of a mechanical turn of mind and was then working on aerial navigation and something that would astonish the world.'

SIGHTING AT DEADWOOD

Subsequently, the *Houston Post* reported that, in Deadwood, Texas, a farmer called H. C. Lagrone had suddenly heard his horse bucking, as if about to run amok. Going outside, he then saw a bright white light circling around the fields nearby and illuminating the entire area before descending and landing in one of the fields. Walking to the landing spot, Lagrone found a crew of five men, three of whom talked to him, while the others collected water in rubber bags. The men informed Lagrone that their airship was one of five that had been flying around the country recently, that theirs was the same vessel that had landed in Beaumont, and that all the ships had been constructed in an interior town in Illinois (which borders Iowa). They were reluctant to say anything more because they had not yet taken out any patents on their machine.

By May 1897, the mysterious airship sightings had stopped. But what lay behind them? Could such airships indeed have been financed by a powerful company in New York and constructed secretly in the wilds of Iowa or Illinois?

This is certainly a possibility. During the late 1890s, numerous inventors in the United States obtained patents for planned airships. But since most of them worried constantly about the possible theft or plagiarism of their designs, they also kept

The German engineer Otto Lilienthal is seen flying one of his biplane gliders, above. Lilienthal was the first inventor to build and fly successful controllable aircraft. He steered by shifting his dangling body and legs from side to side. Although he was killed in a flying accident in 1896, soon after this flight, his successes inspired several other pioneers, including the Wright brothers.

many of their ideas completely secret. Knowing this, many Americans came to believe that Wilson and his friends could well have invented successful airships.

Experimentation in aerodynamics was highly advanced by the 1890s, particularly in Massachusetts (an area having numerous mystery airship sightings) and New York, reportedly Wilson's home city. At the Massachusetts Institute of Technology (MIT), there were plenty of informal courses on propulsion and the behaviour of fluids, relevant to aerodynamics. What is more, by 1896, instructors and students at MIT had built a wind tunnel and were experimenting with it to get practical knowledge of aerodynamics. A man such as Wilson could have attended those courses and then

---

A WAVE OF SIGHTINGS

The American mystery airship wave began in November 1896, as citizens of Sacramento, California, watched a light moving through the night sky. Further sightings were reported from all parts of California throughout the month, with a few from farther north, in Washington State and Canada. A dark shape supporting the light could sometimes be glimpsed, and was variously said to be shaped like a cigar, a barrel or an egg. The airship's motion was slow and undulating, suggesting a wind-blown craft. Some newspapers named inventors who, they speculated, could be responsible. Others floated the idea that the airships were visitors from Mars. Occasionally, airships were seen on the ground: in one such case, two Methodist ministers saw a fiery object taking off as they approached. Three strange beings, very tall and with bald heads, allegedly attempted to kidnap two men on a country road, and then fled in a cigar-shaped craft.

After a two-month lull, the sightings again came thick and fast – this time, from all over the United States and Canada. At one point, each day saw a score of reports coming in – some of them quite startling. A citizen of Michigan, for example, reported that a voice from above the clouds asked him for four dozen egg sandwiches and a pot of coffee – which were duly hauled up to the unseen craft in a scoop. One witness even claimed to have seen a landing ship manned by Oriental-looking crew.

The main 'flap' was over by mid-1897. But later in the year, there were isolated sightings reported from other parts of the world, including Sweden, Norway and Russia.

In September 1897, for instance, some sort of balloon that seemed to have a bright sheen to it was seen by an engineer in the Russian town of Ustyug. Its exact nature was never discovered; but we do know that motor-controlled balloons had indeed been built in England and France by this apparently early date.

gone on to Cornell University in Ithica, New York. Here, by the mid 1890s, it was possible to obtain a bachelor's degree in aeronautics.

PIONEERS IN THE PUBLIC EYE

One of those who gave a series of lectures at Cornell University – noted nationally for its courses in aerodynamics – in 1897 and 1898 was Octave Chanute, the world-famous engineer. In 1896, he had emulated the successful manned hang-glider experiments of the German engineer Otto Lilienthal. The courses at the University included experimental engineering, mechanical and electrical engineering, as well as machine design and construction. Aeronautical texts would have included the Smithsonian Institute's *Experiments in Aerodynamics*, Sir Hiram Maxim's reports on his experiments with engines, propellers and aircraft designs, and the *Aeronautical Annual*, which contained highly innovative contributions from most of the leading aeronautical scientists of the time.

By 1896, the first successful flights of S.P. Langley's flying machines had taken place in Washington, DC; and by the following year, numerous patents for other types of flying machine had been registered. The scientific advances of the last decade of the 19th century were of staggering magnitude, laying the all-important ground work for advanced aeronautical experimentation. So if a particularly dedicated team of scientists did indeed happen to be working on an airship project, it certainly becomes possible that the sightings all over the country that took place during that period were indeed of man-made flying machines.

No more was heard of the mysterious Wilson, however. But the following years saw remarkable further advances in the field of aeronautics. By 1901, the Brazilian Alberto Santos-Dumont had succeeded in flying an airship from St-Cloud, on the western edge of Paris, to the Eiffel Tower and back in less than 30 minutes; two years later at Kitty Hawk, North Carolina, the Wright brothers made the first known heavier-than-air manned flight; and by 1906, the American Robert Goddard had begun his exciting experiment in rocketry. On the last day

The Flyer, above, built by the Wright brothers, takes off on its first brief journey and inaugurates a new age. Four flights were made on that day, 17 December 1903 – the first sustained powered and controlled flights known to history. But could other inventors working in secret have anticipated the Wrights and been responsible for earlier airship sightings?

Louis Bleriot's Number XI flying machine, right, soars above the cliffs of Dover at the end of the prize-winning cross-Channel flight on 25 July 1909.

of December 1908, Wilbur Smith flew 77 miles (123 kilometres) in just two hours and thirty minutes. Seven months later, the French aviator Louis Bleriot became the first to fly across the English Channel, from Calais to Dover.

Since these were all highly publicised achievements, is it possible that even greater advances were being made away from the public gaze? The numerous UFO sightings of the early 20th century and the rapid pace of technological development suggest that this may have been so. In 1904, US Navy Lieutenant Frank H. Schofield – later to be Commander-in-Chief of the US Pacific Fleet – officially reported seeing, from the deck of his ship, three bright lights that were travelling in echelon. They remained above the clouds, and ascended before disappearing. In 1909, numerous unidentified aircraft were reported over Massachusetts. On 30 August 1919, at about 9 p.m., a long black object flew low over Madison Square, New York City, and was witnessed by hundreds of people. The nature and origin of this object were never determined.

In 1933 and 1934, a wave of sightings occurred over Scandinavia. 'Ghost planes' were reported on scores of occasions, frequently appearing or heard overhead in 'impossible' conditions for aircraft of that time. They were described as monoplanes, usually grey in colour. Sometimes their crews could be glimpsed. Often their engines would cut out, and the aircraft would glide for long periods before their power was turned on again – an unlikely feat for conventional aircraft. Sometimes brilliant search-lights would be directed from them on to the ground below.

INVADED TERRITORY

In 1934, the Swedish Air Force began a thorough search of those remote areas from which the 'ghost plane' reports were emanating. Twenty-four aircraft took part in the search, and two of them actually crashed during it. No traces were found of the bases that would be required to support the activities of the intruders, however. In April 1934, a high-ranking Swedish military officer stated in an announcement to the press:

'Comparison of these reports shows that there can be no doubt about illegal air traffic over our secret military areas. . . . In every case, the same remark has been noted: no insignias or identifying marks were visible on the machine. . . . It is impossible to explain away the whole thing as imagination. The question is: Who are they? And why have they been invading our air territory?'

The same questions were by now being asked in Norway and Finland, too, where similar sightings were said to be occurring. But they were never satisfactorily answered either – so that the origin and purpose of these 'ghost planes' still remained utterly elusive.

Aeronautics now advanced from initial crude experiments with wind tunnels in Massachusetts to highly complex rocket research at Peenemünde on Germany's Baltic coast that led to the *V-2*. On the principle that all scientific research resembles an iceberg – in other words, nine-tenths is hidden from public view – the possibility arises that secret research in America, Europe, or both, had led to the construction of machines much more powerful and unorthodox in design than those that were officially put into use. Certainly, it is a fact that, from the First World War onward, more and more technological research was being financed and controlled by governments who were interested mainly in the military applications of craft built as a result of such research.

So the question inevitably remains: is it possible that citizens of the United States and certain European countries had witnessed the clandestine aeronautical experiments being carried out by their very own leaders?

The pace of aviation development accelerated still further during the years of the Second World War. Jet aircraft, radar navigation and detection, ballistic missiles and bombers of unprecedented size all appeared in response to the desperate necessities of the principal combatants. And sightings of equally mysterious craft – such as the balls of light, which became known as 'foo fighters' – then began to enter a new phase, in the skies over embattled Germany.

Only 40 years after the Wright brothers' first flight, air warfare had advanced to the point where rocket propelled, long range ballistic missiles were being prepared for use against cities. In the photograph below, three experimental V-2 rockets stand on their trailers at the Nazis' Peenemünde research centre.

" IT CONSISTED OF A GREAT CIGAR-SHAPED PORTION, POSSIBLY THREE HUNDRED FEET LONG, WITH A CARRIAGE UNDERNEATH... IT WAS BRILLIANTLY LIT WITHIN AND EVERYTHING WAS PLAINLY VISIBLE... THEY WERE JABBERING TOGETHER, BUT WE COULD NOT UNDERSTAND A WORD THEY SAID. **"**

YATES CENTER (KANSAS) FARMER'S ADVOCATE, 23 APRIL 1897

BLIND TERROR IN TEXAS

A TERRIFYING ENCOUNTER WITH A UFO ON A LONELY ROAD IN TEXAS RESULTED IN APPALLING INJURIES FOR THE THREE VICTIMS

Late one chilly evening at the end of December 1980, two middle-aged women and a young boy were driving along a lonely road in the Huffman area of Texas, USA. It was the Christmas season and they were in a festive mood. Suddenly, a bright light appeared in the sky a little way ahead. A few minutes later, the light turned into a huge diamond-shaped object, shooting out from its underside intermittent bursts of fire. This alarming apparition seemed to be trying to land on

'A diamond of fire' – as in the artist's impression, below – was how one of the witnesses described the huge glowing object that hovered over the road, blocking their way. Ringed with lights at the centre, it emitted bursts of fire from its underside that threatened to set light to the surrounding forest.

the road ahead, making it impossible for the three people in the car to continue on their way.

For the occupants of the car, it was to be a terrifying encounter. The intense heat from the UFO burned their skin and the bright light injured their eyes. When the object eventually left the area, a large number of helicopters filled the sky in close pursuit, making a deafening noise that hurt the witnesses' ears. For the three spectators, it was like being caught in the middle of some strange battle for the skies.

Earlier that evening, Betty Cash, together with Vickie and Colby Landrum, had visited several small towns in the Piney Woods area in search of a bingo game; but to their disappointment, they discovered that all such games had been cancelled while the clubs prepared for the New Year's Eve celebration. Instead, the three had settled for an evening meal at a roadside restaurant in New Caney. It was soon after this that the terrifying events of the evening

began. Betty Cash, who was driving her new Oldsmobile Cutlass when the trio encountered the UFO, was then a 51-year-old business woman who ran a restaurant and a grocery store. She was planning to open a new restaurant the very next week. A year or so earlier, she had undergone a heart bypass operation, and had made a complete recovery. Within the next hour, she was to sustain physical injuries more debilitating than any caused by the cardiac surgery.

Vickie Landrum, then 57, was a pleasant, hardworking woman who worked for Betty in the restaurant and also occasionally as a school meals assistant. She was a committed Christian, and did not believe in UFOs or extra-terrestrial life. When the bright object appeared in the sky, she thought it was the coming of the end of the world. Because she expected to see her Saviour come out of the bright cloud, she gazed intently at the UFO. Her reward was not to meet her Saviour, but to sustain severe eye damage.

Colby Landrum, Vickie's grandson, was being brought up by her. He was a healthy and active lad; and at seven years old, he had already earned several trophies for baseball, bowling and other sports. The encounter left him with severe physical and emotional scars. But it is difficult to tell whether he was more frightened by the UFO or by the overpowering noise of the helicopters thundering overhead.

The day had been damp and overcast in Texas. In Huffman, there had been periods of light rain, but by night-time the rain had stopped and the sky had partially cleared. Light from the third-quarter Moon, supplemented by the glow of lights from the surrounding area, made the sky bright and the visibility good. Because the temperature was only 40°F (4.5°C), the victims were wearing coats and the car's heater was keeping the winter chill at bay.

After leaving the restaurant some time between 8.20 and 8.30 p.m., the three drove along Highway FM1485, a road normally used only by people who live in the area because it is so isolated.

The lonely tree-lined road, above, is where Betty Cash and Vickie and Colby Landrum saw the UFO.

A map of the region north-east of Houston, below, shows the Huffman area where the incident occurred. The three victims had dined in New Caney about half-an-hour earlier, and were driving home to Dayton when the UFO appeared on the road ahead.

It was about 30 minutes later when the three noticed the bright UFO above the treetops some distance away. Colby, an alert youngster, was the first to see it. He pointed it out excitedly to Betty and Vickie as it glowed brightly above the trees about 3 miles (5 kilometres) ahead. As they realized the object was approaching the road only a short distance ahead, their apprehension increased. Nevertheless, they hoped to get by in time and leave it behind. But before they could do so, the object had straddled the road, blocking their way.

Vickie screamed: 'Stop the car or we shall be burned alive!' Her warning was probably correct. The object, many times larger than their car, remained hovering at treetop level and sent down an occasional large cone of fire like a rocket blast. In between these blasts, it would settle downwards some 25 feet (7.6 metres) or so, only to rise again on the next cone of fire like some huge science fiction spaceship. Vickie's vivid description of it was that it was 'like a diamond of fire'.

When Betty eventually brought the car to a standstill, the object was less than 65 yards (60 metres) away. It looked as if it were made of dull aluminium, and it glowed so brightly that it lit up the surrounding forest like daylight. The four points of the diamond were blunted rather than sharp, and blue spots or lights ringed its centre. Had the UFO not come to rest over the road, the cone of fire that periodically emanated from its lowest point would have set the forest on fire. In addition to the blast of the fire, the UFO emitted an intermittent beeping sound.

It is not clear whether Betty turned the car engine off, or whether it just died. Whichever it was, the three of them got out of the car to take a closer look at the thing that was blocking their way.

Colby plucked at his grandmother's clothing and begged her to get back inside the car and hold him. Two or three minutes later, in response to his pleading, she did so but told him not to be afraid,

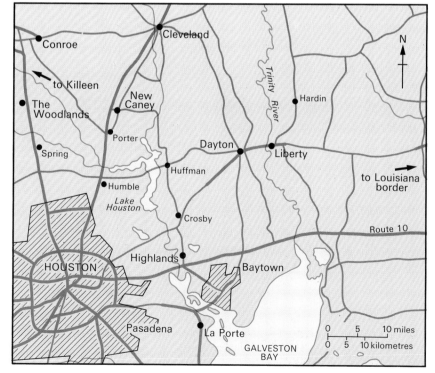

for 'when that big man comes out of the burning cloud, it will be Jesus.'

As Vickie held Colby to comfort him, she screamed to Betty to get back into the car with them. But Betty was so fascinated by the UFO that she walked round to the front of the car and stood there gazing intently at the bright object. She seemed to be mesmerized by it. Bathed in the bright light, she remained standing there although the heat was burning her skin. Even the skin on the finger beneath her ring was burned.

INTENSE HEAT

As the three of them watched the departing UFO, a large number of helicopters appeared overhead. Within a few seconds, the UFO had disappeared behind the trees lining the highway. It was then that the victims became aware of how hot the interior of the car had become. Instead of the heater, they now switched on the air conditioner to make the environment more comfortable.

When the effects of the bright light had worn off, Betty started the engine and they sped off down the darkened highway. After a mile or so of twisting road, they joined a larger highway and were able to turn in the direction of the departing UFO. This was about 5 miles (8 kilometres) and five minutes later. The object was clearly visible some distance ahead, and looked like a bright, oblong cylinder of light.

By this time, the helicopters were spread out over a 5-mile (8-kilometres) area. One main group was still near to the UFO, but moving in an erratic flight path. The others were clearly visible in a steady trail formation. At one point, one of the large 'choppers' flew directly over the car, engulfing it in the roar of its engine and flap of its rotor blades. As they watched from this new vantage point, the victims counted 23 helicopters. Many were the heavy, double rotor type with four wheels and a large housing to the rear. (These were later identified as

A number of small, single rotor helicopters, of the Bell Huey variety, similar to the one shown above, on a military exercise, were seen with the Huffman UFO.

time, they had been involved with the UFO and the helicopters for at least 20 minutes, perhaps longer.

Betty dropped Vickie and Colby at their home at 9.50 p.m. and went home herself. A friend and her children were waiting there for Betty to return; but by then, Betty was feeling too ill to tell them about the incident. Over the next few hours, Betty's skin turned red as if it were badly sunburned, her neck swelled, and blisters erupted and broke on her face, scalp and eyelids. She started to vomit and

CH-47 Chinooks, manufactured by the Vertol division of the Boeing company.) Others were smaller, very fast, single rotor helicopters. These were never clearly identified, but they appeared to be of the Bell Huey variety. There was also a suggestion that there may have been a single, even larger helicopter in the middle of the group.

As soon as the UFO and the helicopters were a safe distance ahead, Betty drove on cautiously. When she reached an intersection, she turned away from the flight path of the UFO and drove towards Dayton, where the three of them lived. By this

Heavy, double rotor helicopters, like the CH-47 shown above, were identified by several witnesses as being present in large numbers at Huffman.

continued to do so periodically throughout the night. Some time between midnight and 2 a.m., Vickie and Colby began to experience similar symptoms, although less severe. At first, they suffered the sunburn-like condition, then diarrhoea and vomiting.

The following morning, Betty was moved to Vickie's home, and all three were cared for there. Betty's condition continued to deteriorate, and three days later she was taken to a hospital casualty department. The casualty staff assumed that Betty was a classic burn victim, and treated her accordingly. They were not told about the UFO until several days later when Colby blurted out to a doctor that he knew what had burned them.

The burns and swelling altered Betty's appearance so radically that friends and relatives who came to visit her in hospital did not recognize her. Her hair started to fall out and she was eventually to lose more than half the hair on her head. When her appearance was compared with the photograph of her taken just before Christmas, it was impossible to believe that it was the same woman. Treatment was further complicated by the fact that Betty and the others had intense headaches and painfully swollen eyes.

The evidence of all the witnesses to the Huffman event was consistent. All were interrogated separately, not only about the UFOs but also about the helicopters.

At the US Army's Fort Hood near Killeen, Texas, press officer Major Tony Geishauser told the *Corpus Christi Caller* that no Fort Hood aircraft were in the Houston area on 29 December 1980. 'I don't know any other place around here that would have that number of helicopters,' he said. 'I don't know what it could be... unless there's a super-secret thing going on.'

At the Robert Gray Field near Fort Hood, a spokesman said they might have 100 helicopters from the Field home in at one time 'for effect', but he claimed they avoided the Houston area. And all other bases in Texas and Louisiana denied they were responsible for the helicopters seen at the Huffman UFO incident.

Is it possible that the witnesses were all mistaken about seeing and hearing the helicopters? The descriptions and sketches provided by Betty, Vickie and Colby indicate that they all clearly saw helicopters of a particular configuration, which is common only to CH-47s. As far as the noise is concerned, witnesses had been accused of wrongly identifying helicopters at an earlier UFO incident on 22 March 1978, which was reported in the St Paul, Minnesota, *Dispatch*.

AMPLIFIED SOUND

That newspaper quoted Dan Meyers, supervisor of the Army Reserve Aviation Support Facility at Holman Field: 'Just one of those helicopters at 1,500 feet (457 metres) would sound like a humming chain-saw from the ground. With five helicopters up there, you would have tremendous amplification.'

In another (possibly related) incident the day before the Huffman event, helicopter activity had also been noted when UFOs were being observed. Dozens of residents of Ohio County, Kentucky, had seen strange moving lights. But when a helicopter arrived in the area, the UFOs left. Again, all military installations denied having any helicopters airborne that night.

But Betty, Vickie and young Colby were not the only witnesses to the strange happenings at Huffman that night. An off-duty Dayton policeman and his wife happened to be driving home from Cleveland through the Huffman area and also observed a large number of CH-47 helicopters in the sky. A man living in Crosby, directly under the flight path, reported seeing a number of heavy helicopters flying overhead, too.

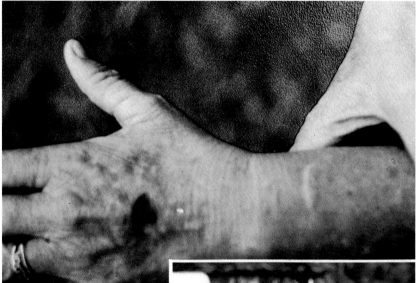

Months after seeing the UFO, the victims were still suffering the results of their encounter. The burn on the back of Vickie's hand is seen above; and a year-and-a-half after the event, her face showed lasting damage, particularly around the eyes, right.

Oilfield labourer Jerry McDonald was in his back garden in Dayton when he saw a huge UFO directly overhead. At first, he thought it was the Goodyear airship, but quickly realized it was some unidentified object. 'It was kind of diamond-shaped and had two twin torches that were shooting brilliant blue flames out the back,' he said. As it passed about 150 feet (45 metres) above him, he saw it had two bright lights on it and a red light in the centre.

The same evening, bakery clerk Belle Magee was at her home, about 8 miles (13 kilometres) west of Dayton, when she saw a bright light in the sky heading in the direction of New Caney.

Certainly, Dr J. Allen Hynek, founder of the Center for UFO Studies in Evanston, Illinois, was convinced the witnesses were not mistaken. 'We are dealing with a real event,' he said, 'but we're not sure if it's a government exercise or a UFO sighting. There is a lot of top secret stuff going on that most people don't know about.' He added: 'Something sure as hell happened. Those women didn't pull out their hair and blind themselves. The connection with the event is clear-cut.'

On the evening of 5 March 1979, Antonio Gonzales Llopis, aged 26, was taking photographs of the island of Gran Canaria, in the Canary Islands, when suddenly he noticed a strange, swirling light in the sky over the sea. A moment later, a huge, dark object hurtled straight up into the sky, surmounting a ball of fire, as shown in photographs *1, 2* and *3*. Llopis pointed his camera at the object, checked its setting, and continued to take pictures throughout the sighting, which he estimated as lasting about three minutes – as later verified by several other witnesses.

The brilliant light surrounding the dark object effectively obscured any detail, but it seemed to accelerate rapidly, somehow shooting through the pattern of lights in the sky. After the object had disappeared, a bright trail and a golden cloud illuminated the sky for half-an-hour, as shown in pictures *4* and *5*. Thousands of people on Gran Canaria reported the incident and many of them took photographs. Some of these even found their way into the files of the Spanish government, increasingly sympathetic towards serious UFO investigation.

The bright lights, *right,* were seen near the major airport of Barajas, 6 miles (10 kilometres) from Madrid, Spain, one night in December 1979. An estimated 10 lights appeared suddenly over Madrid, executed a brief aerial ballet, and then sped off in the direction of Barajas, where this photograph was taken. UFOs seem to be attracted to airports and aircraft, naval bases and ships, nuclear power stations and military establishments of all kinds. Indeed, believers in the extra-terrestrial hypothesis claim that UFOs harbour aliens showing an interest in the hardware of our technology in order to compare our progress with theirs. More down-to-earth observers have suggested that UFOs are, in fact, secret weapons accidentally seen while undergoing trials in the vicinity of military bases.

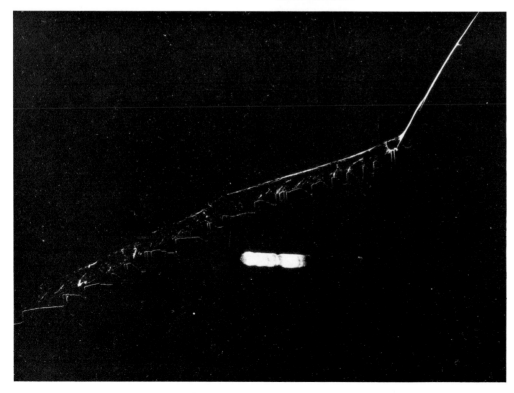

The photograph of a UFO, *left,* was taken near Lakeville, Connecticut, USA, on the night of 23 January 1967, by a 17-year-old pupil from a local boys' boarding school. This was only one of the many sightings of 'bright lights, moving erratically', reported over a four-month period, mainly by boys from the school, although one teacher, and a 12-year-old boy who lived nearby, added their testimony. Condon Report officers Ayer and Wadsworth investigated and went on to study the boy's picture. He described the UFO as 'a bright point of light that blinked or pulsated regularly'. He said it 'pulsated twice', and then disappeared behind Indian Mountain. The investigators left the case open. But could the UFOs have been secret weapons undergoing night trials? Or were they 'nuts and bolts' alien spacecraft?

UFOs OR SECRET WEAPONS?

Top secret research aircraft often outrage normal ideas of how an aeroplane should look and perform. They may even have given rise to UFO reports, some investigators have suggested. How likely is the possibility of such confusion?

The remotely piloted research aircraft (RPRA), above, designed by NASA, would certainly have confused non-expert witnesses to its flights. Its cigar-shaped wing, for example, could be swung to as much as 45° from its normal angle to optimize performance at varying speeds.

The whole upper surface of the NASA craft, right, generated lift. It was launched from a bomber at high altitude.

*The unmanned probe, far right, was not from space but from Westland, a British helicopter manufacturer. The remotely controlled helicopter had rotors 5 feet (1.5 metres) wide and a body 2 feet (60 centimetres) wide which could carry a variety of surveillance equipment.
The feet could leave marks similar to the circular depressions often described in cases of UFO landings.*

Could an extraordinary research project to build flying saucers have been kept wrapped in secrecy since the Second World War? And could our present technology possibly account for the advanced capabilities sometimes ascribed to UFOs?

It is entirely possible that research establishments could have been hidden well away from the gaze of the public and the media. The underground research factories of Nazi Germany, for instance, were gigantic feats of construction, containing wind tunnels, machine shops, assembly plants, rocket launching pads, supply dumps and accommodation for the thousands who worked there; and very few outsiders knew that they even existed. Likewise, the Cheyenne Complex in Colorado Springs, operated by the US Aerospace Defense Command, is virtually an underground city in the heart of a mountain. It rests on giant shock absorbers to counteract the blast of nuclear attack; it is webbed with miles of underground tunnels; it is completely sealed off from the outer world, and invisible from the air – and very few people, other than those who have worked there (all of whom are sworn to secrecy), know what actually goes on inside the establishment.

Equally large and complex establishments for the construction of highly advanced, disc-shaped

The first prototype of the British Flying Wing, right, *was one of several post-war designs that dispensed with the heavy fuselage of conventional aeroplanes. The resulting crescent shape is reminiscent of many UFO reports – including, interestingly, Kenneth Arnold's sighting of 1947 that began the modern UFO wave.*

aircraft could, therefore, exist in other desolate parts of the world, such as the wildernesses of Siberia and North America, the Arctic or the Antarctic.

But while secrecy might prevail during the construction of the machines, it could not be reliably maintained once the machines were test-flown or actually used for reconnaissance or other purposes. It is therefore possible that the relevant authorities simply decided to fly them openly while simultaneously creating an international smokescreen of confusion. The systematic harassment and humiliation of UFO observers and the deliberate inefficiency of official UFO investigations could thus have been the chosen methods of obscuring the issues.

This theory would also go a long way towards explaining such suppressive measures as a US Joint Chiefs of Staff directive of December 1953, which made the unauthorized release of information on UFO sightings a crime under the Espionage Act, and one punishable by a prison term of between one and 10 years or a fine of $10,000. It might also explain what happened to the only scientifically sound attempts to determine the size and capability

of UFOs and whether or not they were intelligently controlled.

Nonetheless, assuming that these saucer-shaped machines were man-made, we are still faced with the second major question: could modern technology achieve the extraordinary capabilities of the craft, as reported by UFO observers, and the equally extraordinary physical appearance that some reported UFO crew members display?

In his book *Ufology*, James M. McCampbell examines in detail the physical properties that UFOs must possess in order to be capable of their reported speeds and manoeuvres. According to McCampbell, UFOs probably use some advanced means of propulsion that, at present, exists only on designers' drawing boards. They might employ ion rockets, for instance, in which the exhaust stream consists of ions (electrically charged particles), accelerated to high speeds by strong electrical fields. Or thrust might be provided by a nuclear fusion pulse rocket, in which a continuous sequence of H-bomb explosions pushes the craft along. Or it might be that the craft use anti-gravity shields – perhaps in combination with one of these forms of propulsion.

Ionization of the air, with accompanying electrical discharges, meanwhile, could account for the glow that so fascinates UFO witnesses. The anti-gravity shield would account for the lack of turbulence and sonic booms associated with the passing of a UFO, and also for the crews' apparent ability to withstand major changes of speed and direction.

SHIELDED FROM GRAVITY

McCampbell claims that the lift-off of a typical UFO would require as much energy as the detonation of an atomic bomb, would cause the body of the machine to heat up to about 155,000°F (85,000°C) and would cause intense radioactivity in the ground and atmosphere – unless anti-gravity shields were used. In this case, a virtually massless body would result, and it would require only modest force for the UFO to achieve enormously high accelerations. This would account for the ability of UFOs to disappear in the blinking of an eye, to come to a very abrupt stop, to hover in the air and to make seemingly impossible right-angle turns.

In this context, it should be noted that, as far back as 1965, at least 46 unclassified projects concerned with gravity were being undertaken in

CITY SIGHTING

Photographs ought to provide good evidence of a UFO sighting, but they are not always so reliable. Sometimes, for example, a UFO can appear on a picture when the photographer did not actually see one at the time. Sometimes, too, the object appears differently on the photograph from the way that the observer remembers seeing it. So evidence from genuine pictures, too, is often ambiguous.

Sightings of true UFOs over London, as over any major city, are a rarity. Many reports are made, but these often prove to be misidentifications of lights in the sky. This is hardly surprising, considering the great volume of aircraft flying over the city on the way in or out of Heathrow airport. There are also many other aircraft flying over at great height and, at night, satellites reflect the rays of a sun already well below the western horizon. Few who report sightings in fact fulfil the condition of having seen a UFO at close range – that is, near enough to be classified as a close encounter of the first kind.

One sighting towards the end of 1966, however, may have fulfilled this condition and the report was reinforced by photographs that seem to show remarkable changes in the shape of the images.

The day of the sighting was Thursday, 15 December 1966. It was one of the shortest days of the year: the Sun set at 3.53 p.m. The weather was unpleasant – misty, dull and damp, with drizzle, rain and low cloud – and maximum visibility was 2 miles (3 kilometres).

At approximately 2.30 that afternoon, Anthony Russell was standing by the open window of his flat in Lewin Road, Streatham, south-west London. Lewin Road is at the southern end of Streatham High Road and just west of Streatham Common. The window by which Russell stood faces approximately north-north-west. A keen photographer, he was testing for resolution two new 2 X converters for his Zenith 3N single lens reflex camera (focal length 135 millimetres increased to 270 millimetres by one converter). During the testing, Russell was aiming the camera at the gable of a house on the far side of Lewin Road, about 28 yards (26 metres) from the lens. The camera was loaded with 35-millimetre Gratispool colour film.

The first photograph taken by Anthony Russell is shown right. There is a hint of an efflux from the base of the object on the right. The bar seen on the gable of the house across the road supports a chimney that is off-camera.

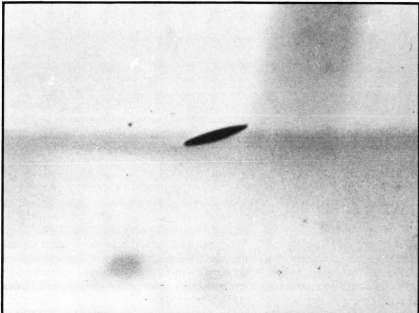

It is reasonable to assume that the eight blank frames were due to the speedy rolling-on of the film between shots in the excitement occasioned by an incident that lasted two minutes at most. The following is a reconstruction of those two minutes.

After the initial swift descent and abrupt halt of the UFO, Russell took his first two shots. He used the single converter that he had been testing, set at 1/125 second (f/5.6). He then hurried away from the window and fitted the second (Panagar) converter. With a focal length now of 540 millimetres, he set the exposure at 1/25 second (f/11). Returning to the window, he saw the object 'stand on end' and present its full circular shape to him before turning

Suddenly, Russell became aware of an object in the sky falling, stopping dead, and then drifting slowly earthwards with a pendulum-like motion. Amazed at first, but rapidly collecting his wits, he 'slapped the camera to infinity' and began snapping. He thought he got 12 photographs. The last two shots were taken as the object moved away, at first slowly and then at much greater speed.

The witness had enjoyed only limited contact with UFO literature before, in as much as his father had designed a cover for the book *Flying Saucers Have Landed* by George Adamski and Desmond Leslie. Russell did not think much of the book, however; and, after meeting Adamski, thought even less of the subject. But his scepticism received a jolt as he stood photographing the strange object.

Russell left the rest of the film in the camera so that he could take photographs at Christmas and sent it away for processing after the holiday period. In the meantime, he told a few friends what had happened. They were inclined to laugh off the incident, but he felt it was worth investigating. He did not wish for the publicity a newspaper might have brought him, but he was not sure who would be genuinely interested. Fearing he would get short shrift from established bodies such as the Royal Astronomical Society or the Royal Aeronautical Society, he looked through the telephone directory under the word 'flying' and happened on *Flying Saucer Review*. He wrote to the magazine, explaining what he expected to be found on his pictures when the film was returned, and the magazine arranged for R.H.B. Winder and Gordon Creighton to help in an investigation once the pictures were available for study.

From the start of the investigation, there was a measure of disappointment for the witness, as only three of the 12 frames came out well. A fourth – the last to be taken – revealed a dim shape that had little definition. Russell was puzzled by the object's apparent changes of shape because he did not recall seeing such changes. He remembered seeing only changes of aspect.

Russell's second photograph, top, shows the UFO edge-on which emphasises its disc shape. The expert who examined the photographs for fraud could not explain the strange shadow effects on this shot.

The third photograph, above, caught the UFO in a slanted position, perhaps in the ascent since it was taken just before the object sped away. When enlarged, the picture revealed a marked efflux to the left.

❚❚SUDDENLY, RUSSELL BECAME AWARE OF AN OBJECT IN THE SKY FALLING, STOPPING DEAD, AND THEN DRIFTING SLOWLY EARTHWARDS WITH A PENDULUM-LIKE MOTION. AMAZED AT FIRST, BUT RAPIDLY COLLECTING HIS WITS, HE 'SLAPPED THE CAMERA TO INFINITY' AND BEGAN SNAPPING. **❚❚**

through 90° about a vertical axis until it was edge on. The UFO then started to move to his right. During all that period, Russell shot only two successful snaps, though he could not have known this at the time. It was during the moment of movement to the right that the third good picture was captured. Then the fourth followed as the UFO accelerated away. By the time Russell reset the camera for the next shot, the object had gone.

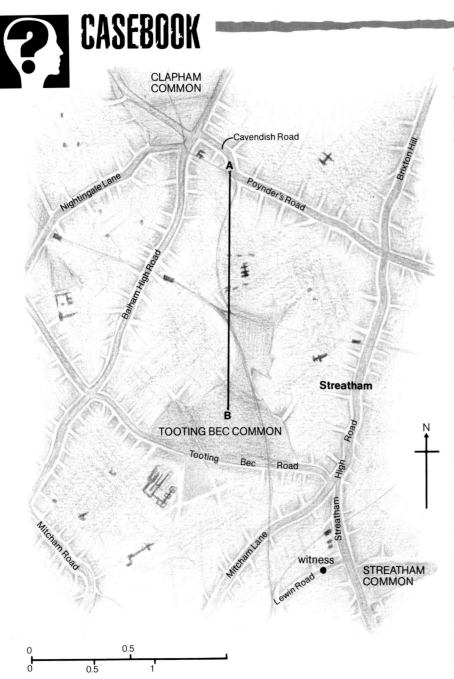

object might have been anything up to a mile (1.6 kilometres) away. In the photograph, there is a hint of an efflux streaming to the right from the base of the UFO – a feature that was more clearly seen when the image had been enlarged and viewed on a projector.

Winder pointed out that the silhouette image of the UFO on the first photograph bore a remarkable similarity to the shape drawn by Police Constable Colin Perks after his sighting of a UFO at Wilmslow, Cheshire, on 7 January 1966, at 4.10 a.m. PC Perks was checking the back door of a shop when he heard a high-pitched whine. He turned and looked over the car park behind the shops. There he saw a solid-looking object – stationary – some 35 feet (10 metres) above the grass of the meadow beyond the car park. It was about 100 yards (90 metres) from him. Perks said the UFO's upper surfaces glowed steadily with a greenish-grey colour, a glow that did not hide the definite shape of the object. He said the lines in his sketch 'represented rounded, but fairly sharp changes in the profile, matched by shading in the glow'. Nowhere could he see openings like portholes or doors. His estimate of a diameter of 30 feet (9 metres) for the base was based on a mental comparison with a 30-foot (9-metre) bus. After about five seconds, the object moved off east-south-east with no change of sound. Then it disappeared.

Russell's other photographs brought no further comparisons to mind. But in the second picture, there are strange shadow effects, particularly one that slants away in the '7 o'clock' position. Hennell could offer no explanation for this.

The third photograph seems to have been blurred either by the motion of the object – it was beginning to move away – or by camera shake. An efflux effect is also noticeable to the left of the object. This in fact was quite pronounced when the picture was enlarged.

Judging from Russell's position and the 2-mile (3-kilometre) visibility limit, the object appears to have been somewhere on a line from a point on Tooting Bec Common to Cavendish Road.

After investigation, the researchers handed the transparencies to *Flying Saucer Review*'s photographic consultant, Percy Hennell. After examining them, he made plate negatives from the first three, and stated that they were 'genuine photographs of an object in the air'. He could detect no signs of the transparencies having been tampered with. Later, the transparencies were projected on to a 12-foot (3.5metre) square screen. Close inspection revealed nothing suspicious.

The investigators ascertained that the object was not luminous, and that it would have been virtually impossible for the witness to distinguish any colour, owing to the fact that it was being viewed as a dark object against a light background. Russell merely suggested it might have been maroon.

The first photograph shows the gable of the house opposite Russell's flat with a near-horizontal bar to the right that acts as a support for a chimney that is off-camera. Winder estimated that the bar would have been at an angle of elevation of 10° from the lens of the camera. Russell thought the

The map, seen top, shows the area in which Russell spotted the UFO over Streatham. The object appears to have been somewhere along line A – B.

The drawing, above, was made by PC Colin Perks after he saw a UFO in Cheshire about a year before Russell's sighting. The two reports are strikingly similar.

A contact at Heathrow airport told the investigators that the object was not observed on the radar screens, but it is possible that it missed the radar sweep by virtue of its plummeting fall between sweeps.

The Ministry of Defence (Air) was asked about weather balloons on 15 December 1966. The answer was that four were released in south and south-west England earlier than the sighting, but that they would not have migrated to the London area. The precise nature of this urban sighting remains unidentified.